D1598370

PRAISE FOR *BURNED*

"Julie Bee's *Burned* delivers actionable strategies for entrepreneurs to conquer burnout and thrive. Finally, you will be(e) burned no more!"

Mike Michalowicz, Author, *All In* and *Profit First*

"*Burned* is a business owner's no-BS guide to burnout. The Introduction gives permission to jump into a chapter where you have a need, making *Burned* a resource you can keep coming back to. I thought that was genius and made it easy to digest. AWESOME book!"

Ron Nussbaum, Founder/CEO, BuilderComs

"Julie Bee's *Burned* is a groundbreaking work that tackles the often-overlooked issue of burnout among business owners. With a blend of research, real-life stories, and actionable advice, this book is an essential read for anyone looking to conquer burnout and achieve success."

Bill Stainton, CSP, CPAE, 29-time Emmy Winner, Hall of Fame Speaker

"From the first page to the last, *Burned* is a powerful and essential guide for every business owner navigating the exciting but sometimes unstable waters of entrepreneurship. In an era where burnout is an all-too-common companion on the path to success, this book emerges as a beacon of hope and wisdom. Reading this book is not just an investment in your business; it's an investment in your future, your happiness, and your health."

Trish Saemann, CEO/Cofounder, GoBeyond SEO

"Finally! A book written for business owners to help acknowledge and normalize something that happens to all of us: BURNOUT. Throughout *Burned*, Julie helps us understand what we're experiencing, shows us how to battle through, and outlines how to keep moving forward by embracing the gift of what she aptly describes as the 'silver lining' of burnout."

**Angie Stegall, Executive Coach, Certified Martha
Beck Wayfinder Life Coach, Certified Forest
Therapy Guide, Certified Sparketype® Advisor**

"*Burned* is an absolute must-read for business owners: a book that finally addresses burnout from an entrepreneur's unique perspective. Beyond the firsthand experience, what sets this book apart is its practicality. It's not just a book; it's a reference guide that lets busy business owners access the insights they need, exactly when they need them."

**Renee Hode, Director, Small Business and
Entrepreneurship, South Piedmont Community College**

"My only complaint is that this book wasn't written years ago when I, like so many business owners, found myself burned out and ready to walk away from it all. They say business is a marathon, not a sprint. *Burned* is a treasure trove of practical tips, giving the structure we need to balance progress with endurance. Mandatory reading for all business owners."

Mark Drager, CEO and Cofounder, SalesLoop

"*Burned* is a must-read for all entrepreneurs. You don't need to be suffering from burnout to benefit from reading *Burned* because it is full of strategies you can implement today to prevent burnout altogether. This is a book I will come back to many times to read specific chapters."

Michelle O'Connor, President, O'Connor Insurance Associates

"Julie has created a manual showing you how to actually run a business that doesn't wear you down every few months. I feel like a better entrepreneur having read this book. *Burned* should be required reading for founders and entrepreneurs!"

Chenell Basilio, Founder, Growth in Reverse

"Julie brings to light the challenges around one of the hardest issues that business owners and leaders deal with—burnout. While most businesses are led by people with a myriad of special skills, the ones who get the furthest are the ones who learn to manage burnout before it gets too far. *Burned* will show you the best ways to navigate this tricky pitfall and get through it stronger than when you started."

Taylor Evans, President, Rust Belt Recruiting

"*Burned* is a no-nonsense guide to identifying, framing, and dealing with burnout. We *all* need this. Business is moving faster than ever, and there's so much pressure. This is a great resource for anyone launching a business, looking to stay in business, or pivoting in their business."

Lynn Power, Cofounder and CEO, MASAMI

"Julie Bee provides great insight to all business owners and leaders through her book, *Burned*. We've all been there—the 2 am wake-up call worrying about payroll, revenue, our people, and our clients. Julie maps out the warning signs and gives you specific action steps to avoid them. Read this book and don't get burned."

Kathleen Quinn Votaw, Author, Speaker, and CEO, TalenTrust

"Having advised thousands of small business owners over the past decade, I have learned that burnout is one of the top silent killers of passion for business owners. Julie's book addresses different aspects and stages of burnout, providing guidance on identifying red flags, addressing problems, recovering, and leveraging burnout for future success. If you are at risk of burnout in your business, you need to read this book."

Michael R. Moore, Regional Director, SBTDC

"Julie Bee is an expert on teaching business people about many topics—particularly things not taught in traditional business schools. Meeting Julie and working with her was one of the best things to happen to me in the last couple of years. Read this book!!"

Steve Rosenberg, The GSD Group, and Author,
Make Bold Things Happen: Inspirational
Stories from Sports, Business, and Life

BURNED

BURNED

How Business Owners Can Overcome Burnout and Fuel Success

JULIE BEE

Matt Holt Books
An Imprint of BenBella Books, Inc.
Dallas, TX

Burned copyright © 2024 by Julie Bee

Matt Holt is an imprint of BenBella Books, Inc.
10440 N. Central Expressway
Suite 800
Dallas, TX 75231
benbellabooks.com
Send feedback to feedback@benbellabooks.com

BenBella and *Matt Holt* are federally registered trademarks.

Printed in the United States of America
10 9 8 7 6 5 4 3 2 1

Library of Congress Control Number: 2023048753
ISBN 9781637744901 (hardcover)
ISBN 9781637744918 (electronic)

Editing by Katie Dickman and Lydia Choi
Copyediting by Jennifer Brett Greenstein
Proofreading by Jenny Bridges and Cape Cod Compositors, Inc.
Text design and composition by Aaron Edmiston
Cover design by Brigid Pearson
Printed by Lake Book Manufacturing

For Dixie & Bobby Bee

Mom, *thank you for being my first mentor and teaching me how to take the wheel.*

Dad, *thank you for being my first coach. I finally listened and started shooting those shots.*

I won the jackpot in the parent lottery.

Love ~ Your Baby Girl

CONTENTS

PART III: MOVING FORWARD AFTER BURNOUT

BURNED

INTRODUCTION

On a Friday morning in August 2021, I woke up with heart palpitations and chest pain. I was sweating and nauseated. My blood pressure was 156/110. My pulse was in the 130s. I thought I was having a heart attack. All I could think on the way to the emergency room was, "Am I going to die?"

At the time, I had too much on my plate. In the emergency room that day, I had a lot of time to think about my choices. To think about dying. To think about living without the stress I had carried for too long.

When I finally saw the doctor, he told me my heart was fine and that I had experienced a panic attack. He reminded me that panic attacks are one of the body's ways of warning us that something is very wrong. He gave me the standard advice of "do less and take better care of yourself" and sent me home with orders to follow up with my other doctors.

I was the very picture of business-owner burnout. To strangers and acquaintances, it appeared that I had it all together. But my closest friends and advisors knew I was burned out—they'd been telling me to take care of myself. I knew I was burned out, too.

All the signs were there—why hadn't I done something about it?

Something had to change. I needed to make space in my life. I also needed a system to follow. A process that would help me recover from this burnout and prevent future ones.

I will finish my personal story in the epilogue, but this realization set the wheels in motion for writing this book. It turned out I had a burnout system already—it just wasn't documented, and therefore I wasn't following it. After reviewing my own past situations, hearing stories of how others experience burnout, doing research, reflecting on my own mental-health journey, and having countless conversations with a diverse population of business owners about burnout, a documented system for us to battle this beast was born.

This is *Burned.*

ABOUT THIS GUIDE

My goal in writing this book is to first normalize burnout for business owners. The hustle and grind of owning a company is part of our daily lives, and it can cause burnout. Balancing this dynamic is a challenge, to say the least.

Burned gives you a process for all stages of burnout, providing a systematic way to identify, address, recover, prevent, and leverage it. This book will define many elements of burnout, including how and why it is different for founders and entrepreneurs than for other groups of individuals.

I wrote this for all of us business owners. It recognizes that our work and personal lives are difficult (if not impossible) to separate, so both are incorporated in this book. It gives us all some easy-to-use language for when we need to address burnout, and all within the context of business ownership.

I know founders and self-made CEOs—we often just want the facts and information we need to make informed decisions. If you've ever read a book and thought, "Just get to the point already," this book is for you. You won't find a lot of filler in these pages—it's mostly direction to act on. While I do use some stories, in those cases they are the best way to illustrate the lesson.

After reading the book and working through the action steps in each chapter, you'll have a plan for every element of the overwhelming stress you feel when in a state of burnout. Along the way, you'll begin to see the silver linings of burnout. Make note of those silver linings and any "aha" moments. Toward the end of the book, I'll share with you a process to leverage them in a way that has a positive impact on you and your business.

Professional Disclaimer

I'm not a doctor, therapist, counselor, medical provider, attorney, or human-resources professional. I'm a business owner who has had several rounds of burnout, and I've created a process for it. I'm sharing that process in this book. Nothing I share should be taken as medical, mental health, legal, and/or human resources advice.

READING THIS BOOK

Business owners will be at various stages of burnout when they start reading. Some may have experienced it in the past but don't feel burned out now. Some may be in the middle of a highly disengaged state and need a path out. Some may be ready to leverage their past scenarios to fuel their success. Here are some guidelines on how to read this book.

Jump to Any Chapter at Any Time

This is not a book you have to read in order, though you can read it that way if you wish. It was written with the busy entrepreneur in mind, and I hope it becomes something you reference as often as you need.

This book is broken down into three parts: "Understanding Burnout," "Battling Burnout," and "Moving Forward After Burnout." Each part contains chapters relevant to those overall themes.

I've summarized each chapter below to help guide you in determining where to begin reading.

Part I: Understanding Burnout	
Chapter 1: Burnout Is Different for Business Owners and Why This Matters	Read this if you think, "I'm a business owner; I chose this path. Never-ending, overwhelming stress is part of my job." This chapter shares how burnout is different for business owners and why we need to discuss it in this context.
Chapter 2: Burnout Red Flags	Read this if you want a process to measure and track indicators that signal you're on a path to burnout and learn how to course-correct before you reach it.
Chapter 3: Burnout Triggers	Read this if you want to regain control of how you respond to people, places, and situations that trigger overwhelming stress before they cause, or worsen, burnout.
Part II: Battling Burnout	
Chapter 4: Make Space to Address Burnout	Read this if you want to address burnout without slowing down. This chapter confronts the reality of our busy schedules and offers alternative solutions for making space that are not dependent on time.

Chapter 5: Identify Burnout Types and Timelines	Read this if you don't know how to tell if you're "just" stressed or actually burned out. This chapter also defines the types and timelines of burnout in the business-owner context.
Chapter 6: Determine Causes and Isolate Your Burnout	Read this if you need or want to continue working while you are burned out and/or if you need help determining the underlying causes of your burnout.
Chapter 7: Address the Problems Burnout Creates	Read this if burnout has created problems in your business and/or personal life and you need to quickly stop those problems in their tracks before you can focus on recovering personally from burnout.
Chapter 8: Recover from Burnout	Read this if you want a process to recover from burnout that you can incorporate into everyday life. This chapter focuses on actions that will work for you within thirty days.
Part III: Moving Forward After Burnout	
Chapter 9: Prevent Future Burnout	Read this if you have experienced burnout in the past and want to build a four-step process to prevent it in the future.
Chapter 10: Embrace Burnout	Read this if you want to know why we should embrace burnout instead of running from it. You'll learn to embrace it and play with its fires, which builds the foundation to leverage it.
Chapter 11: Leverage Burnout	Read this if you are currently not burned out and want to leverage your past burnout lessons to fuel your growth and success (however you define them).
Chapter 12: The Gift of Burnout	Read this if you want to learn about the ultimate gift of burnout. A summary of the entire book is also included at the end of this chapter.
Epilogue: What Happened After the Emergency Room?	Read this if you want to know the conclusion of the emergency room story I introduced in the first paragraphs of this book and how I ultimately leveraged that burnout experience.

Get Your Free Workbook Guide

In many parts of this book, I'll ask you to document certain elements. I've created a free workbook that you can claim with your email address and proof of purchase. Please go to this web page to get your workbook:

https://www.thejuliebee.com/burned

Once we verify your purchase, we'll email you a free copy of the digital workbook.

Now let's look at one assumption I've made. Then you'll be ready to roll.

Important Assumption About Teams

Throughout this book, I assume that you have a support team in your business and in your personal life. At work, your team might be one employee or contractor, or a strategic business advisor (like a coach or consultant). In your personal life, your team might include a significant other, best friend, or family member.

You may be asking, "But what if I don't have a team in my business or at home?"

That's a great question, and you are not alone. Even if you do not have a team, you will benefit from reading this book. It will also highlight the importance of building your support teams.

You can buy support if you have financial resources—employees, strategic advisors, babysitters, and so on. You can look at the people in your life and see if any of them can be on your support team. Sometimes asking for help on social media or texting a group of people may help you find the resources you seek.

If you don't have a support team right now, start building one. It's important even on the good days to have people you can rely on. It's crucial on the bad days, especially when you're burned out.

This book is a no-nonsense, no-fluff, desk-reference kind of book that will help business owners understand and work through burnout. I hope you find the book easy to navigate and the content immensely helpful.

Let's dive into *Burned*.

Part I

UNDERSTANDING BURNOUT

CHAPTER 1

Burnout Is Different for Business Owners and Why This Matters

As business owners, we often struggle to admit when we are burned out because we think that if we're not okay, our business isn't okay, and our employees won't be okay. If we aren't okay, there are many other things that can quickly become unstable. We must also be careful about how much we share and with whom because telling the wrong people we are burned out can backfire.

That's exactly why I believe it is important for entrepreneurs to have a support team with whom they can safely discuss burnout. It's also why learning how to have a conversation about it without stressing everyone else is important. Leaders need to know that it's okay for them to not be okay.

Articulating this, finding support, and then addressing it are challenging for most entrepreneurs. There's still a stigma around burnout for company founders—almost a "you started this company, so you asked for this never-ending stress" mentality. It doesn't have to be this way, and I have written this book to try to help change the narrative.

In this chapter, I share several reasons why it's important to discuss business-owner burnout and how it differs from that of other groups. I also share a few reasons why it is important for us to have a place to acknowledge and discuss it.

Chapter Overview

Section	Summary
Why It's Important to Discuss Burnout	Four reasons why it's important for this conversation to happen.
Why Is Burnout Different for Business Owners?	Six reasons burnout is different for business owners, and why those reasons cause burnout.
When Stress Becomes Burnout—the Tipping Point	How feeling stuck and engaging in self-sabotage can indicate that a business owner is burned out.
The Silver Linings	How business owners can see the upside of burnout by changing their narrative around it.

WHY IT'S IMPORTANT TO DISCUSS BURNOUT

Burnout Is Unavoidable

I've written an entire book on this topic because I believe burnout is unavoidable for business owners. I've experienced it several times in this role. I know many others who have experienced it several times as well. And the data supported this premise even before we endured a pandemic.

A Gallup poll from 2020 indicated that before the COVID-19 pandemic, 38 percent of female and 45 percent of male small business owners (SBOs) had daily stress. During the pandemic, those numbers jumped to 62 percent for women and 51 percent for men.[1] As we know, stress can eventually lead to burnout. It's a leading indicator in this conversation. And in a September 2022 survey of 1,295 SBOs, nearly half (48 percent) said that they were either currently experiencing or had experienced burnout within the last month.[2]

Based on these two reports, along with my conversations with business owners over the years, I feel strongly that entrepreneurs will face burnout at some point in their careers. Each experience is different—some are more severe than others. Some, in hindsight, were preventable. A few were not.

For example, a CEO friend of mine had the following events take place over the course of one month: Four members of her leadership team notified her they would take maternity leave over the course of the next year. If that weren't enough, during one week of that month one of her parents and one of her spouse's parents were *both* diagnosed with Alzheimer's.

There was absolutely nothing she could do to control those events, and yes, she burned out. It was almost inevitable that she would; most of us would under those circumstances.

I have spoken with hundreds of entrepreneurs over the years. Almost every one of them has a significant burnout story. Mine was the trip to the emergency room. Others have had divorces, emergency surgeries, business closures, and heart attacks. I consider myself lucky.

Burnout is unavoidable, and once we accept this, we can learn to leverage it.

This book will help you learn how to prevent the burnout you can prevent, and how to plan for unavoidable instances to lessen the impact when they happen.

We (Think We) Don't Have Time to Address Our Stress

Most people do not realize how hard being a business owner is until they become one. The hustle and grind are real. The whole blood, sweat, and tears thing? Very real. Entrepreneurship can consume all our time if we let it. It's very easy to put our heads down, do the hard work, grind through it, and tell ourselves we don't have time to address our stress. I know I've said, "You don't have time to be stressed" to myself in the past.

I fully recognize that sometimes the hardest work we do as business owners is putting our work away to make time and space to address our stress. For example, rescheduling an important work meeting to go to the doctor is hard work for a business owner. Taking a walk instead of making those five phone calls that might lead to a sale is hard work for a business owner.

What we eventually learn, often through burning out, is that more hustle, grind, and hard work to power through stress are not the answer. We may think we don't have space to address our stress, but we do—and I'll outline how you can find it in chapter four.

We Are Master Negotiators

As entrepreneurs, we're also fantastic negotiators when it comes to our own well-being.

"I'll exercise tomorrow, but tonight I have to get this work done."

"I'll reschedule that doctor's appointment because I feel fine today—just a little stressed."

"I'll cook dinner tomorrow evening; tonight, I just need to grab something at a drive-through."

"Our biggest client has an emergency; I only need to work two days while we're on vacation."

All those statements are my own, but I know they resonate with some of you. We think we can easily compromise our well-being to keep up with our work, but if we don't address our stress, the consequences will take far more resources and time when we are forced to face them.

The reality for entrepreneurs is that addressing and reducing stress is a necessity. Burnout lurks around every corner; addressing stress before you turn that corner is a crucial skill to acquire.

Take care of yourself to prevent or lessen the impact of burnout, or it will take care of you (and not in a good way).

Sometimes Self-Care Isn't Enough

When I talk with business owners who are burned out, there is a common thread among them. Many of them already practice self-care. They take vacations. They've hired a lawn-maintenance person at home. They exercise.

Even the best efforts for self-care sometimes are not enough. So what can we do?

For entrepreneurs struggling with never-ending stress, there is often no level of escaping (vacations or breaks) or throwing money at a problem (hiring at work and at home) that will fix it.

When I searched for answers online, I found much of the same generalized advice we've heard for years. Eat right, sleep well, take a vacation, meditate, and set better boundaries. That's all good advice, much of which is echoed throughout this book.

But what happens when you already have a self-care routine and it isn't enough? That's where I find many business leaders—they prioritize their well-being but need more help.

Summary Table

Burnout is important to discuss because . . .	Reality Check
It's unavoidable.	Studies support this statement. Anecdotally, I have spoken with thousands of business owners, one on one, over the years. So far, only *five* said they've never experienced burnout.
We think we don't have time to address it.	Do we have time to deal with the consequences of burnout?
We are master negotiators with our own time and self-care.	"I'll take care of myself tomorrow; today I must focus on work." That statement could instead be, "I'll take care of myself *today* and finish that work tomorrow."
We are already practicing self-care.	Many burned-out business owners are already doing some form of self-care. Sometimes our existing self-care routines aren't enough.

How does a business owner practice burnout prevention? What does prevention even look like? Most of the solutions out there focus on recovering from burnout, but few offer insights into addressing the source of the problem.

None of the advice I've found offers a system specifically for business owners that includes prevention with measurable guideposts. I needed that system, so I created it. There's more to come later about this system, so stay tuned.

Now that we've talked about why burnout is so important to discuss, let's look at why it's different for entrepreneurs.

WHY IS BURNOUT DIFFERENT FOR BUSINESS OWNERS?

First, I want to say that "different" doesn't mean better or worse, easier or harder. A stay-at-home mom's burnout can be worse than a founder's burnout. A corporate professional can experience levels of burnout that are higher than a visionary's level.

I can speak authentically to burnout for business owners being different in part because I've experienced that overwhelming stress both as a corporate professional and as a caregiver. Those experiences were dramatically different from what I've gone through as the president of my companies.

I've been an entrepreneur for over fifteen years. Prior to that, I worked in small businesses for four years, working closely with the companies' owners. I've lived this burnout, I've seen it happen to CEOs, and I've spoken with many more about their experiences.

Based on that perspective, I've identified several reasons why business-owner burnout is different from what others may experience. Not all these reasons exist in every case, but there is usually at least one.

Reason #1: We Are Financially Responsible for Three to Four Entities

When I think about how burnout is different for company owners, this is one of the biggest factors that comes to mind. Business owners are financially responsible for multiple entities, all the time.

First, we are financially responsible for the business. If we do any number of things poorly (from sales to hiring staff), the business entity may not have enough money to survive.

Second, we are responsible for at least part of our personal income. If the business doesn't make (enough) money, the business owner doesn't get a paycheck.

Third, taking it a step further, we often feel financial responsibility for our team. How we manage and lead the business directly affects the personal finances of everyone who works for us.

It's Not Just Me . . .

This financial responsibility hit Frank Schwartz, founder of G3L Leadership and LEC Media, especially hard and contributed to his burnout. He says, "I was so tired of the chase that was required to make payroll. These people were depending on me for their financial security, and that was a lot on my shoulders." There was also the overhead that came with a new commercial office space for his larger company. Layered on top of that, Frank was also the primary income earner at home. Those burdens are part of why business owner burnout is different from that of other professions. There's so much financial responsibility beyond yourself, and that can certainly increase your likelihood of burnout. I'll share more of Frank's experience throughout this book.

In some cases, business owners are also responsible for the financial success of their clients. Financial planners, CPAs, bookkeepers, sales consultants, and marketing consultants come to the top of my mind when I think about this category.

There are three to four entities for which entrepreneurs feel financially responsible every single day. That is a burden unlike any other. Many company owners I know are the main income earner at home, too, which amplifies this dynamic.

Why This Causes Burnout for Business Owners

Finances cause stress for most people. That stress is multiplied for founders because they are financially responsible for many others beyond themselves.

But one of the main reasons this financial burden causes so much stress, leading to burnout, is that many business owners define their success by money. If they aren't making enough money, they deem themselves unsuccessful. I agree that can be a goal—you are in business to make money. But you are also in business for other reasons. We'll get into this in future chapters.

If you run a business and you're not making enough money to support those entities, it makes you feel bad about yourself personally, and that makes asking for help very hard. It's hard to say, "I don't have enough money right now." That is a very hard, embarrassing statement to make. I know because I've said it.

What's important to note in this part of the book is the "right now" part of that statement. Because it is a "right now" statement. It may be true today, but it probably won't be true a few months from now or this time next year. Most entrepreneurs are resilient people who figure out how to solve problems.

"I don't have enough money right now" is fine to say. Focus on the "right now" part—it isn't "forever."

At the end of the day, money is an important part of business. It's also one of the biggest stressors for business leaders. It can create a sense of pride or a sense of worthlessness. Multiply those thoughts and feelings by three to four, and that's what makes overwhelming stress about money different for business owners (and why that stress can cause burnout).

Reason #2: It's Lonely at the Top

It's true—it is lonely at the top. This is true for high achievers who are the best in their field. It's true for CEOs. It's true for the single mom making all the decisions for her family. It's true for business owners—including solopreneurs.

So first, let's take a moment and pat ourselves on the back for being part of that badass club—because you are badass. You must be to take on the responsibility that comes along with great power. But why is being lonely at the top different for business leaders?

It's especially lonely at the top because not many make the same climb we do.

If you've been burned by sharing your worries before, it's also easy to become paranoid about who is around you. You begin to question motives. You wonder if the people around you would stay if you weren't at the top.

When you're at the top, you also need several filters. You filter what you say to employees and your leadership team. You filter what you say to your significant other. You filter what you say to your friends. They often don't have or need the full context about what's going on in your business. You're constantly filtering what you say about your business and to whom you say it. That can become exhausting, but it is a necessary skill of being at the top.

Why This Causes Burnout for Business Owners

When you're an entrepreneur, the lonely-at-the-top feeling hits you differently because it is harder to find trustworthy people who really understand what you're going through. There's a small pool of sympathetic cars. You're filtering what you say and to whom. Every decision has a consequence, and you're often making those decisions alone. You are the face of those decisions and the consequences that follow.

That's an isolating and lonely experience.

Support Is Fundamental

When I asked Meghan Lynch, CEO of Six-Point Creative, about being lonely at the top, she knew the feeling all too well. She shared with me how she prevents that feeling, which has helped her recover from burnout as well as prevent it.

"For me, finding peer groups has been an absolute game-changer. When you're in a room of peers who just get it, they get the business ownership aspects of your life like nobody else understands."

Meghan is a member of the Women Presidents Organization (WPO), as well as a graduate of the Goldman Sachs 10,000 Small Businesses program. Meghan says, "Going into those groups, it's just the safest space. I've told people in those groups things about business that I haven't even told my husband. There's a connection there that is irreplaceable." Meghan goes on to implore business owners who have not yet found a safe space of peers like this to do so as soon as possible. "There are so many different ways to get into these kinds of groups, but you need it. It is fundamental."

When we're at the top, there's an expectation of showing up for certain roles no matter what. We can ask others for help, but we can't simply stop doing our jobs. We can hire people to take on roles in our business, but we're still responsible for the results of their work. We can outsource when needed, but we can't outsource our role as the founder, creator, and visionary. We can even hire a CEO, but we're still the company's owner (until we sell or walk away).

There are parts of a business owner's job that no one else can do.

Those elements—the isolation and the expectation of showing up—make for a very lonely environment at the top. All of which can cause burnout.

Reason #3: Our Reputations Are on the Line

Burnout is different for business owners because of the impact it can have on their reputation. In business, your reputation is everything. There are some chief cooks and bottle washers for whom this is more true than for others, but for those of us who have started a company, our reputation can make or break our business.

We are incredibly invested in our businesses and in those who support them. We will put almost anything on the line for them, including our personal reputations. That's a big part of the reason burnout is different for business owners. A lot of pressure and emotions are tied to both our personal reputation and our company's reputation, and this cuts both ways.

Take as an example an HVAC or car mechanic, a business where the work should speak for itself. If the business owner is known to be unreliable or a jerk, their personal reputation will negatively affect the company. Even if the company does excellent work and the owner doesn't deliver the work themselves, the owner's personal reputation can still greatly influence the company's success.

This reputation dynamic goes both ways. If the business has a bad reputation, that will trickle over to the business owner. The business owner could be the most compassionate human with outstanding integrity, but if the quality of the product or service they provide is subpar, that becomes their personal reputation and their company's reputation in their community.

When it comes to reputation, it is extremely difficult to separate our company's reputation from our personal one.

We want to reach our own definitions of success and be seen as successful business leaders in our communities. Our personal reputation and how it's connected to our business—that situation is different for business owners than it is for others.

Why This Causes Burnout for Business Owners

We're taught from the start that our reputation in business is everything. We live in a world where one bad review online can wipe out a career's worth of good work. Not only can it wipe out a company's good name, but it can also cause a business owner's reputation to go from gold to garbage very quickly.

That's a lot of stress to carry every day. If one bad review comes in—depending on the industry—it becomes a fire to put out. That is enough to put an already overburdened entrepreneur into burnout.

And finally, the reason our concerns over our reputation can cause crushing stress is that, often, our reputation becomes entangled with our self-worth. If you get a bad review, or if a client cancels their contract, it's a slippery slope from "my business made a mistake" to "I'm a really bad entrepreneur." The mistake needs to be addressed, but it doesn't mean you're bad at owning a company. It just means a mistake happened. Most of you know this feeling because you've been there and done that before.

We are not our business, yet we are simultaneously very much so. Balancing that inescapable truth can cause burnout.

Reason #4: We Have Something to Prove

Most business owners I know have something to prove—to themselves and, often, to others.

Businesses are often started because an individual wanted to be their own boss. Or someone had to start a business because they couldn't find another job and wanted to prove they could make it on their own.

Sometimes a creator starts a business because they know they have greater potential and they want to challenge themselves to fulfill that potential. And sometimes a visionary starts a business with an idea that everyone else thinks is weird, but they want to prove that their idea works.

And this "something to prove" mentality often continues beyond the startup stage.

"The Kind of Tired Sleep Can't Fix"

Frank Schwartz's burnout story starts out like it does for many other owners—trying to achieve our culture's definition of success.

"In 2016, my business [LEC Media] was doing well, and I thought I was unstoppable. I had a strategic plan that I was actively working to become an eight-figure business. I had identified businesses to acquire across the Southeast. The first acquisition happened in Charlotte, North

Carolina." In hindsight, Frank would realize that this first acquisition was the beginning of his burnout.

Frank had consultants telling him what the eight-figure plan would entail and how grueling it could be. But as Frank puts it, "Arrogance really kicked in here, and I remember thinking, 'Dumber people have done this and made it work. I'll figure it out and be fine.'" What happened after that first acquisition was a fast descent from the top of the world to what felt like the universe systematically dismantling everything Frank was working toward for his business.

Frank's business experienced a heavy downturn. "It was that scenario where a lot happened all at once. One of our largest clients cleaned out their marketing department, firing all its vendors, including us. That hurt, but I thought, 'We'll be fine; we'll pull through,'" recalls Frank. Then another client decided to hire marketing staff internally, ending the relationship with Frank's company. Even then, Frank thought, "That sucks, but we'll make it. I'm Frank Schwartz; I've got this."

From there, things only got worse. Other clients left. Frank had burned through every bit of cash his company had to keep things afloat. As he puts it, "There was a point in time where I couldn't buy a client." And then burnout set in. Frank says he remembers driving out into an empty field, just staring out the window and asking himself, "What have I done? What on Earth is going on?"

"I was the kind of tired sleep can't fix," Frank recalls. "I just couldn't do business ownership this way anymore."

Eventually, Frank did overcome this burnout. He came to terms with the fact that he was the problem and sought coaching to help get back on track. He changed the model of his company, downsized, and built a life outside work. Frank did ultimately recover from and then leverage this burnout.

Why This Causes Burnout for Business Owners

Underneath all of this is a theme of proving your worth to yourself and to others. No one wants to disappoint the people in their lives. No one wants to be proven wrong.

That's a lot of pressure for business owners. Half of businesses fail in the first five years.[3] Even non-business owners know that statistic. We're told from the start we have, at best, a fifty-fifty shot. That's fuel for most business owners—it gives them a chance to prove themselves.

Imagine selecting your field of study in school and being told that you only have a 50 percent chance to make it in that field. Or, before you decide to become a caregiver, being told that you only have a 50 percent chance at being successful as a caregiver five years from now. Deciding to take on those roles anyway—that's what new business owners do every single time they start a business.

This mentality of proving that statistic wrong, of being the one who no one thinks will make it but then does, exists in most self-made CEOs. A fight to survive, no matter the cost.

That pressure is part of what drives us; it's part of what allows us to work hard and stay focused. But it is also part of the reason burnout is different for us. From the beginning, we know there's a high likelihood that we'll fail, that we're risking everything to prove others wrong. And we do it anyway.

Reason #5: We Fake It 'Til We Make It

We are great at hiding our problems. We regularly "fake it 'til we make it." There is a time in business when this is a survival tactic, usually when you're getting started. After all, no one wants to be your first client or customer. So yes—early on, sometimes we business owners do need to fake it 'til we make it.

But there's also a time when it is harmful to fake being okay and to choose not to share the truth with at least a few people in your life (including yourself). "Fake it 'til you make it" can leave you feeling worse off than your true scenario is. It's only by sharing with trusted parties—by no longer faking it—that you can have that revelation. One reason I find owners hide their problems comes down to pride and ego. There's nothing wrong with being confident and having pride in our work, in what we've built. But sometimes that pride and confidence, that ego, can cause us to "fake it" to our detriment.

The challenge is that opening up about what is really going on requires vulnerability. Being vulnerable even with the people we trust about our stress and our challenges is difficult for some of us. I think that comes from a fear of being viewed as a failure. But our struggles do not mean we've failed. Burnout or other major challenges in business do not equal failure.

We tend to hide our stress levels and our challenges. Even if the people running a company have a support network and resources, it can take a lot for them to share how stressed they are or how big a problem has become.

For some, particular problems may signal to them that they're not successful. Anything negative about money, like debt or lack of cash flow, can be hard problems for business leaders to share. People challenges, too, are especially difficult to share because we're afraid we'll be viewed as a leadership failure. These two items—money and people—can become a big part of how a business owner defines their own success.

Also, we often hide our problems because we don't want to burden others. I understand this—no one wants to be a Debbie Downer. But if you think sharing your challenges might bring another person down, I strongly encourage you not to make that assumption. That other person may want to help you but not know how. Or they may be facing a similar challenge in business and also need support. Don't assume they don't want to hear your concerns. If you're unsure, you can always ask for permission to discuss a challenge. That might sound like "Hey, I have this challenging thing going on with cash flow—can I talk with you about it for a few minutes?" If they don't want to discuss it, they'll tell you.

Why This Causes Burnout for Business Owners

When you hide your problems, or fake it 'til you make it, that causes stress. That stress has to go somewhere. If you don't have anyone to talk about it with, that stress turns inward on you and becomes a never-ending state of fake it 'til you make it. Feelings take up space just like physical objects do. If you don't make an outward space for your stress, usually through talking about it with someone, that's a recipe for burnout.

Finally, some founders (I am one of them) are eternally optimistic. We chase success, however we've defined that for ourselves, and minimize the threat of the challenges we face. We believe in ourselves and our mission and vision, sometimes to a fault. But this allows us to shrug off our problems because we really believe that if we can just get to that one thing we seek, then we'll be able to deal with all those underlying problems. Don't get me wrong—a healthy level of optimism is a good character trait to have in this field. But there also needs to be a level of reality. We need both an awareness of our problems and a sense of the underlying stress our worry over those problems can cause.

I've had a few smaller burnouts because of my optimism without realism, so now I make a point to share some of the more stressful issues I carry at any given time with the more pragmatic people in my support network. This helps me make sure I'm not being blindly optimistic and has helped me avoid burning out.

Reason #6: There's a Lack of Resources and Direction

The final reason entrepreneurial burnout is different is that there is a lack of resources for addressing and preventing burnout, as well as a lack of direction to the right resources. As the boss, we are often the one charged with seeking resources or finding answers for others and for ourselves. But when we have intense, overwhelming stress, finding resources to deal with that stress can be too much of a burden. So we continue on our path, carrying that stress, until we reach burnout.

There's no sign that says, "Business owner well-being help found here." There's no manual about who to contact when you have certain types of stress. There's no compassionate boss who brings attention to your stress for you. There's no company resource guide with a number to call. And seeking out resources and direction for yourself requires at least a little vulnerability, so if you aren't willing to open up, this task becomes even harder.

You also may not know what kind of help you need, but it's still on you to figure that out and then to go get it. It sounds straightforward when you're not burned out or when you're only a little stressed. But usually by the time you get to the point of looking for help with never-ending stress, you're too late. What often happens here is business owners will throw money at the things that are causing them stress, but it doesn't fix the problem. That happens because they either don't know what the real problem is or don't have the capacity to find the best answer for themselves (or both). And this can cause even more stress.

If you share your stress with others, many will suggest you take a vacation. I believe that is the worst advice you can give an overwhelmed business owner. First, a vacation may cause more stress. The thought of taking time off hits first. Then, the fact that you may not be able to take time off for, or afford, a vacation (which comes with a layer of guilt) may show up. Finally, planning a vacation is stressful for many people.

But let's assume you can take that vacation. When you take a vacation in response to problems causing stress, you are running away from those problems, not addressing them.

What happens when you come back from vacation? Will you enjoy your vacation, or will you be worried about the problems back home while you're gone? For business owners who are stressed out, a vacation can help them get away and clear their heads for a bit, but they'll need help dealing with the stressor when they get back. Vacations can help a business owner gain clarity, but they don't fix burnout or stress. To be clear, I'm pro-vacation. But if that's the only direction a business owner gets when they share that they are burned out, they are asking the wrong people for advice. Vacations do not fix burnout. There must be a better plan.

Why This Causes Burnout for Business Owners

When you're burned out and have nothing left to give anyone, it can feel impossible to seek help. It adds pressure to an already overwhelming situation. Business owners are given the advice to have a banking relationship before they need a banking relationship. I think the same is true when it comes to overwhelming stress and talking about our problems: have those resources and a support network established before you need them.

Sometimes guilt creeps in here as well. I've been in that place and asked myself, "Why can't I just figure out who to ask for help?" It's tough to realize that you need help but don't know where to turn.

Another reason seeking help when already stressed can cause burnout is a lack of resources to implement the help that is available. I can go to Google easily and search for "resources for burned-out entrepreneurs." That's not the problem. The problem is that many of those resources require an investment of thousands of dollars or there's a long waitlist to get into the program. The same can be said about seeking private therapy, even if you have health insurance coverage. What if you cannot afford the coach or the therapy? Who do you talk to?

There are a lot of free and low-cost resources available, but those are harder to find. They're even harder to access—there's often a lot of paperwork involved. If you are approved for free or low-cost help, then you usually have to wait quite a while to start getting that help.

So you've got a business owner who's already stressed out about something, already feeling guilty about dealing with that stress, and now has to navigate the above system? Even if you have financial resources, you still have to identify the right source of help and then go through its system and process. And if you don't have financial resources, it's much, much harder to access any help at all. That alone can be a full-time job.

I share all this to illustrate why finding help when you are already stressed and on the verge of burnout can be the tipping point. What if you select the wrong resource? You can see why this alone can either cause a stressed-out business leader to decide not to deal with their stress at that moment or cause them so much additional stress that they actually burn out.

Have your resource plan in place *before* you need it.

When you have to create your own plan without a structure or template, that task can be daunting. The good news is that this book provides a system that will help create that plan.

Another reason seeking resources can cause a business owner who is already stressed out to completely burn out is the high-achieving nature of most business owners. They tend to want to fix things quickly, get it right the first time, and refuse to give up. There's a tendency to dig their heels in even more when they're told they can't do something. So telling a high-achieving CEO that they can't afford a certain solution or that they can't find the right solution or that the solution they chose actually failed them can lead them into a tailspin.

These high achievers also have specific needs when it comes to resources and direction. If you fall into this category, it's just something to be aware of as you look for help. Don't let your need for achievement outweigh your need to find the right help for you.

Summary Table

Reason	Why It Causes Burnout for Entrepreneurs
We are financially responsible for three to four entities.	Finances are stressful for most people. Multiply that weight by three or four, along with potential guilt, and this kind of stress can easily lead to burnout.
It's lonely at the top.	There's no one else above us to ask for help, we shoulder expectations, and there's only a small pool of others we can trust enough to share our situation.

Our reputations are on the line.	Our reputations are everything; one bad review online can tarnish our reputation for the world to see, and our reputations are often entangled with our self-worth.
We have something to prove.	The pressure of proving ourselves to others or proving someone was wrong about our idea puts us in a fight to survive, no matter the cost.
We fake it 'til we make it.	We are great at hiding our problems, sometimes our pride blinds us to reality, and eventually that can boil over into burnout.
There's a lack of resources and direction.	With limited resources on how to address burnout and a lack of direction on how to access and implement them, it's very difficult to address our problems.

Now that we've covered why it's important to discuss business owner burnout and how it differs from that of other professions, let's talk about the moment when stress becomes burnout.

WHEN STRESS BECOMES BURNOUT— THE TIPPING POINT

Most of the time for owners and founders, stress happens first. There's a tipping point when this stress changes into burnout. It looks different for everyone, but there are three common elements that show up for most business owners.

First, business owners find themselves ignoring their gut instincts about their businesses. Second, they feel a level of "stuck" that they've never felt before, and they see no end in sight. Finally, when the two items above are combined, business owners often get to a point where they want to burn their business to the ground (figuratively).

Let's unpack this point when stress turns into burnout for business owners.

Listen to Your Gut Instincts Before It Becomes a 2 × 4

Angie Stegall is an executive coach and Wayfinder (she's coached me for over a decade—this book wouldn't exist without her). Her description of when stress turns into burnout provides a great visual example. As Angie puts it, "It starts with a whisper, or maybe a little knowing. That whisper or knowing is telling you something needs to change. You either listen, or you don't and things stay the same.

"If you don't listen, that whisper turns into an annoying buzz, like a mosquito flying around your head. If you still don't listen at that point, that annoying buzz turns into a shout. And if you're still not listening to the shout? It turns into a 2 × 4 piece of lumber that smacks you around."

The moral of the story here? Listen to your gut instincts—and give them some space to explore. Otherwise, you'll end up in what Angie calls "holy unrest," which results from doing what you think you're supposed to do instead of what you actually desire to do.

Feeling Stuck in Your Business and Hating It

When the business owner's stress turns into burnout, the business owner will feel stuck. They will feel trapped by their business. The passion they once had will turn to dread. Their responsibilities will become a burden. This is a common story among company owners who have experienced burnout.

You desperately want to go on autopilot but cannot. You want to just show up to work, clock in, put your head down, do the work, and then go home. But that's not an option for most business owners.

They become less productive and get no enjoyment out of work, which hurts their self-esteem. They know they need help, but the little energy they have is spent on work. They don't have the energy to find (or even ask for) that help.

At this point, they're usually okay admitting they are burned out, but it's hard to find the energy to address it. And then comes the big flip—they get to the point where they hate the work they do and the business they've created, and they cannot keep going. I've seen one of two things happen at this point for proprietors—myself included: their body sends a big warning signal or their business shuts down.

Usually, it's the body warning signal that happens. As I've mentioned before, that "let's get it done" attitude many of us have usually prevents the business from shutting down completely.

I've heard many tales of trips to the emergency room from business owners. It happens at this flip. They feel so stuck in their business that, if they haven't prepared for this situation, it takes getting to a place like this to gain clarity and realize something must change.

Your Burnout Influences Those Around You

When a business owner is burned out, they don't really talk about what's going on when asked because they don't want to burden others. But when we don't talk about those challenges out loud, we end up shouldering all those problems in silence. And shouldering problems and challenges in silence makes the burnout worse because we feel even more trapped by our business. It's a vicious cycle.

When we get to this level, what we can't see is the environment our situation creates for those around us—the people we lead. Which is probably a blessing, because noticing the effects on others would create an additional level of stress on top of our burnout and cause even more problems.

Here are just a few ways your burnout trickles down to the people who follow you:

- If you're out of the office for an extended period, what happens to your team? Who does your work? You don't know the answer, and neither does your team—that's scary.
- It can create a workaholic culture where there's no work–life harmony for your team.
- Employees also burn out. If you think dealing with your own burnout is bad, dealing with an employee's on top of yours is even harder.
- When you're burned out, everyone around you works more but is less productive and innovative.
- What if you had 60 percent of your team constantly out sick and the other 40 percent short-tempered all the time? Is that a place where you'd want to work? Probably not. That's a tongue-in-cheek example, but it's also a possibility if the business owner lets their burnout take over their business.

That's not a pretty picture of a workplace. We are entrepreneurs, but we are also leaders. For me, realizing that my burnouts were creating burdens for my people forced me to take a long, hard look at how I was working.

Am I hitting any nerves? Striking a chord with you yet? Do you see yourself or your team in some of these statements? That's okay—take a deep breath—that's what I wanted to do. This is important and challenging work, and I'll give you a process for it in later chapters.

Burn It to the Ground—Self-Sabotage

If there was any doubt that a business owner was burned out, the final tipping point often includes some self-sabotage. I've seen this range from ignoring sales calls to closing their business.

The fantasy usually involves some version of walking away from the business altogether. Closing it, firing all your employees, and just walking away from the organization that you've worked so hard to build.

Kind of ironic, isn't it? There's a raw connection to the term *burnout* because it succinctly describes what we often feel when we're at this point: we literally want to "burn" the company "out" of existence.

Why Do Business Owners Have This Thought?

I believe we get to this point when the business has burned through all we have to give it. When you get to that point in your business, it's hard to pull yourself out of those thoughts. You can get into some dark places, too. Depression and anxiety can creep in; paranoia, grief, feelings of being a failure show up as well. I've visited all of those spots on my entrepreneurial adventures, and I know I'm not the only one. It's okay; we'll get through it together.

This is why it's important to embrace that burnout is a part of the business-owner journey. Instead of running away from it, if founders face it head-on, they'll be better able to cope with it—to course-correct before their burnout actually does burn their company to the ground.

Your business affects a lot of people around you—your staff, your family, key vendors. But it doesn't affect anyone more than it does you. Sometimes, when things feel really bad, it's easier to walk away than it is to run toward the fire.

However, there is a reason to face burnout head on: the silver linings.

THE SILVER LININGS

There are almost always silver linings throughout a business leader's burnout journey.

When you have a more open and positive relationship with it, when you have a plan for it, you can often see the silver linings more quickly.

Almost every time that I've been burned out, I've come out the other side with invaluable lessons that made me a stronger, more successful, and more compassionate human.

It is up to you to address your unbearable stress, to take measures to avoid those emergency-room trips and to also have a plan for when you do get into a dire state.

One thing I know for sure is that if you run a business, you will experience burnout. And you have the power to write the narrative before it happens. You have the power to change what it means for you, your family, and your business. If you handle your burnout well, the disengagement and fatigue you feel in that state will no longer be something lurking in the darkness around every corner.

Burnout will become something you're prepared for, can address more quickly, and can even benefit from once the dust has settled.

That's exactly what this book will teach you to do in the following chapters.

ARE YOU READY TO DO THE WORK?

You just learned that, yes, it is okay to not be okay. What you've read in this chapter highlights how business owner burnout is different and why it's important to discuss.

The rest of this book is the system to address it. Some of the work will ask you to think about things differently than you have before. Some work will require new habits. Some of the work will look like one question that can be answered in two sentences that won't take much time to write. Implementing your answers, though—that's the hard work.

All the work requires you to be honest and open with yourself.

As with most things in life, you get out what you put in. The same rule applies with this book. If you're ready to dive in, keep reading.

CHAPTER TAKEAWAYS

It is important to discuss business-owner burnout for a variety of reasons. One of the biggest reasons is that burnout is unavoidable. Another important reason is that there are limited resources specifically for founders; this book is now one of those resources.

- Burnout is not a competition. What we as entrepreneurs experience is not better or worse than what other groups of individuals experience. It is simply different, and there are six reasons why.

- Burnout happens when normal stress turns into never-ending, unbearable stress. There are three factors that entrepreneurs experience at the tipping point when stress becomes burnout.

- There is a silver lining in most burnouts—the lessons we learn from them. What we do with those lessons, how well we leverage them, is up to us. The rest of the book helps you form the building blocks to make the most of those lessons.

CHAPTER 2

Burnout Red Flags

Knowing your burnout red flags and how to work with them may be the most important step to keep stress from turning into full-on burnout. This can help you both prevent burnout from happening and address burnout if you're currently in it.

Red flags are actions you take, habits that form, and characteristics that manifest that may lead to burnout. We all have them. They usually show up as changes to our normal routines or behaviors because we're too busy or too stressed. For example, skipping your annual physical for a client meeting or lashing out at a family member because you cannot do what they need in that moment.

I once screamed obscenities at my spouse for planning a birthday party for me. It was not a surprise party, but somehow I was surprised when it came time to leave for it. I know—horrible, right? If you know me personally, you'll probably find this shocking.

While the party was on a weekend, I was angry because I had planned to work that weekend (one of my red flags). In hindsight,

I was clearly burned out from work. In that moment, though, I was yelling and basically throwing a temper tantrum. That's very far from my normal behavior. I've been with my partner for seventeen years, and we've had fewer than ten "yelling" arguments in that time (and we've been through some very rough times together). Neither of us argue through yelling.

If I feel the need to raise my voice toward a loved one, that's a burnout red flag.

The good news about these red flags is twofold. First, red flags can help you identify a potential burnout that is around the corner and course-correct to prevent it. Second, these red flags are your own behaviors and actions (not someone else's), so you have an immense opportunity to control how you address them.

Throughout this chapter, try hard to not label these red flags as good or bad. My main goal is for you to become aware of your personal red flags and identify a way to measure them.

In this chapter, you will learn about the building blocks of burnout prevention—your red flags, baselines, and danger zones. For those burnouts that are unavoidable, learning these building blocks will help you lessen the impact. This chapter can help you see burnout coming and mitigate the fallout or prevent it altogether.

Chapter Overview

Section	Summary
Step 1: Identify Two Red Flags	A definition of red flags and a guide for how to identify two of your own.
Step 2: Measure and Track Your Indicators	How to determine your baseline, danger zone, and burnout levels for each red flag.

Step 3: Back to Baseline—Stop the Slide	How to correct course if you are in your danger zone.
Step 4: Increase Awareness and Accountability	How to remain aware of your red flags and be accountable for addressing danger zones.

My Personal Red Flags

Some of my red flags, in addition to raising my voice in arguments, include not sleeping well for more than a week, being unable to recall important conversations at work or at home, consuming alcohol, not focusing, working both days on a weekend, and canceling checkup or follow-up doctor appointments.

One of my biggest red flags to indicate I'm headed toward burnout is when I repeatedly say, "I just need to get through / get past [fill in the blank]." It isn't the milestone or goal that is the burnout red flag; it is saying or thinking "just get through / get past." When this happens, I immediately evaluate where I am in my danger zone by looking at my other known red flags. And if my support team hears me saying this, they draw attention to it as well.

Burnout red flags come in many forms for entrepreneurs. Your red flags will differ from those of other founders. Remember the good news, though: these actions, habits, and traits are things you can control.

Let's get into a process to help you identify your red flags and keep them from spiraling into full-on burnout.

STEP 1: IDENTIFY TWO RED FLAGS

This part of the work is a deep dive, and the last thing I want is for this to cause you more fatigue and disengagement. If working through the following steps with two red flags seems overwhelming, start with just one. Aim for progress, not perfection.

Red flags tend to be repetitive behaviors, thoughts, or things we say during times of stress. They can also include stopping regular self-care behaviors. We'll begin the work of identifying your personal red flags by looking at your personal history.

Wearing Flip-Flops to Work

In Frank Schwartz's case, he did several things that indicated to anyone around him that he was burned out. He recalls, "I was the guy who wore a suit to the office every day. But for a year and a half, I was showing up to work in flip-flops and shorts." He would also sit in his office and watch Netflix. He couldn't come up with new ideas. Frank is usually an idea factory. But for a year and a half, he had none.

Going forward, Frank learned to identify these three items—how he dresses at work, what he does at work, and if he's coming up with new ideas—as red flags to help him prevent burnout. He also shared these red flags with his support system and asked them to keep an eye out for these actions.

Think back to your past burnouts and look for patterns. Pay particular attention to actions you were taking or avoiding. Look for elements you can measure—for example, hours of sleep, how often you see your friends or family, and the number of days each week that you enjoy work. These are all easily tracked.

Also pay close attention to the thoughts you said to yourself and the words you said to others during those times. Find a mix of actions (or inactions) and thoughts you had, or words you said, during those times. Those are red flags and can also be measured.

Remember, you can download the workbook at **https://www.thejuliebee.com/burned** to keep track of your work.

STEP 2: MEASURE AND TRACK YOUR INDICATORS

Most business owners don't go from "everything is great" to burnout overnight. The space in between those extremes is your danger zone. You identified one or two red flags in the previous step. But before you can use this awareness to prevent a slide into full-on burnout, it is essential for you to know what your "normal" or baseline is for each red flag, as well as your burnout level.

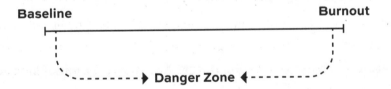

Going forward, I'll use the term *baseline* instead of *normal* when discussing red flags. All of these markers will vary from person to person, even if they share the same red flag.

This step is best illustrated by sharing a few personal examples.

Decision-Making

A common red flag for us, from sole proprietors to CEOs, is a struggle to make decisions. Here is my personal example.

A decision to invest $2,500 or less usually takes me at most two weeks to make—that is my baseline. When it takes me a month or more to decide on investing $1,000 into my companies, I'm at my burnout level.

My danger zone is between those two points. The closer I am to my baseline, the farther I am away from burnout.

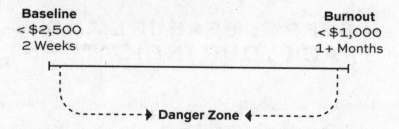

Baseline
< $2,500
2 Weeks

Burnout
< $1,000
1+ Months

Danger Zone

As I mentioned, going from great to complete disengagement does not happen overnight. There's usually a progression. When you understand that the space between these measurable red flags is a danger zone, you can course-correct before you get to full-on burnout.

Let's look at two more examples.

Social Withdrawal

When I'm burned out, I withdraw from friends and family. There are a few ways I measure this.

In my baseline zone, I am a happy-go-lucky extrovert five out of the seven days in a week. During those days, I want to talk and text with my friends, call my mom, and meet with other company owners. I'm still at my baseline even if I have two days a week when I'm grumpy or just off my game. I am human, after all.

However, if I'm socially withdrawn for four weeks in a row, I'm burned out. My wife will see me lying on the couch, face down. My friends won't hear from me at all. Emails will pile up and I won't respond. Those are some of my other measurable red flags.

While everyone gets to have a bad day (or even a bad two weeks) from time to time, I know I am burned out if any of the above happens for four weeks in a row.

My danger zone is between my baseline—extroversion for five out of seven days a week—and four weeks in a row of social withdrawal.

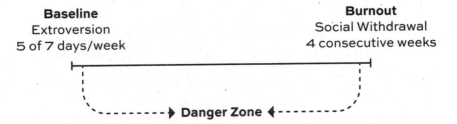

Sleep

Poor sleep is one of the most common red flags I hear about from entrepreneurs. It's one of mine as well. My baseline for sleep is seven hours at night during the week, and around nine hours on weekend nights. This is very measurable.

Some of us wear smartwatches that track sleep automatically; I do not. I often fall asleep reading a book, so I track my sleep by mentally noting the time on my reading device when I get into bed. When I wake up, I note what time it is when I put on my watch (one of the first things I do in the morning). I then record my sleep and wake times in an app on my phone.

When I'm burned out, I get five hours of sleep (or less) on a weeknight. Because we all have those days and weeks when we struggle to sleep, I go a step further to identify my sleep danger zone. If I get five hours or less of sleep on weeknights for two consecutive weeks, I'm burned out.

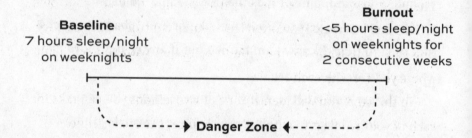

There are weeks, of course, when I get five to six hours of sleep each night for a very good reason. This is why it's important to have more than one red flag to keep tabs on. If you have a newborn at home, or a sick pet, or you are sick yourself, your sleep will be negatively affected. If you pay attention to your other red flags, you'll have a more complete picture given your current life circumstances.

At this point, you have measurable baseline and burnout guideposts for a couple of red flags.

If you are in your danger zone between those guideposts, you can course-correct. Because you've applied some unit of measurement to your red flags, you now know exactly how much space exists between where you are now and your point of burnout. You can also gauge how deep you are into your danger zone, which will help you in the next step: getting back to baseline.

STEP 3: BACK TO BASELINE— STOP THE SLIDE

The good news about red flags is that, because they are your own actions and behaviors, you often have a lot of control over them. Getting back to baseline requires you to be honest with yourself about where you are with each red flag.

In this step, you will identify one or two actions you can take for each of your red flags to stop the slide and get back to baseline.

Let's continue with the three examples from above: decision-making, social withdrawal, and sleep.

Decision-Making

Here are some ways I personally address the red flag of not being able to make decisions:

- I ask for help with making the decision from a key team member.
- I go for a walk and talk to myself about the decision.
- I break down the decision that needs to be made into smaller parts and make mini decisions.
- I get lost in a hobby.

As soon as I recognize I'm in my danger zone, I implement some or all of these actions to address the red flag and get back to my baseline.

Social Withdrawal

When I'm experiencing this red flag, I have several actions that help me get back to baseline:

- I get off the couch—even if it's to sit in a chair. Face down on the couch is not a place I want to be, ever.
- I text my friends. Texting is easier than calling when I'm in my danger zone.
- I tell my wife I'm experiencing social withdrawal and ask for help getting out of the house.
- I make plans to see a friend or my family in person. I almost always feel better when I hang out with them.
- I *do not* jump right back into the emails or work phone calls because I know that tends to put me back on the couch, face down. I triage those and return only to the most crucial ones, giving myself permission to let the others wait until I'm closer to baseline.

Which actions I implement will depend on where I am in my danger zone. But I have a list of actions I can implement, and any of them helps course-correct and prevent or address burnout.

Sleep

I have a few things I do to get back to baseline with sleep. Getting more sleep is often easier said than done, so my action steps go beyond that:

- I plan naps for the early afternoon. If I can't get my seven hours during the night, I'll make up for it during the day.
- I don't make plans for the next morning of work. I know that's counterintuitive and goes against a lot of advice about productivity. But for me, if I know I have something important to do in the morning, it makes it hard for me

to sleep at night. When I'm in my danger zone, I clear my morning schedule as best I can, and I don't make definite plans about what I hope to get accomplished the following morning.

- I get ready for bed earlier in the evening than I normally do.
- I turn off alarm clocks. I know this isn't possible for everyone, but it works for me. I go to bed with no pressure on myself about getting up by a certain time.

Once you have this list for each red flag, you can implement these actions to get yourself back to baseline and prevent burnout.

STEP 4: INCREASE AWARENESS AND ACCOUNTABILITY

One element that comes up when I talk about danger zones and stopping the slide is accountability. While some red flags are outwardly recognizable by others, many aren't. Awareness of our red flags has to start with each of us.

How to Remain Aware of Red Flags

For some red flags, you will need to stay vigilant about tracking them. For example, I keep track of my sleep daily so I can easily see how I am doing with that potential red flag. Do I remember how many hours I slept three weeks ago? No, but I can easily find the answer in my app.

For other red flags, you will know where you are without needing to track anything. I know right away if I'm socially withdrawn because it's a clear and visible opposite of my baseline behavior.

The important part here is that you identify some ways to maintain an awareness of a red flag as exactly that and not only as an action or a "thing you do." For example, how slowly I make decisions when I'm in my danger zone isn't only "how I do things," it's also a personal red flag for me to monitor.

To maintain this awareness, some use sticky notes or whiteboards. Some entrepreneurs keep a reminder in the note-taking app on their smartphone. It's especially important to do this for the red flags we tend to forget are red flags, the ones that sneak up on us, or the ones that are easily written off as normal behavior.

Preventing and addressing burnout starts with awareness. Often, accountability is also needed.

Accountability with Red Flags

It's okay to need help remembering that certain actions are red flags—to ask for accountability in this area. If the reminders you create for yourself aren't enough, you may need the help of others. Whether you turn to a friend, a loved one, another business owner in a mastermind group, a coach, or a therapist, ask for help with accountability. You don't have to share every red flag with your chosen accountability partners—you can be selective in how you ask for help recognizing the red flags. It isn't their job to fix the red flag for you, but you can ask them for help in alerting you to it. This will help you be more accountable for your own awareness and provides backup when you need it most.

You can also communicate with people in your support system about how they can help you prevent burnout (or get out of it).

You already have a list of actions to counter each red flag. Ask your accountability partners for help making sure you do (at least) one of them.

For example, I'll tell my wife I'm stressed and to be on the lookout for "face down on the couch" time. I'll ask her to draw attention to it if she sees it even just one time. I'll also communicate with her that I need to get out of the house more frequently, and she'll know that's a new priority until I get back to baseline.

At work, I might go to that key employee and ask them to help make some decisions, letting them know I need to shift that responsibility to them for a bit. If I delegate work to a team member, I often help them reprioritize the work they already had on their plate to accommodate the new tasks I'm delegating to them. That way, they do not feel overwhelmed. But by having that conversation, I work my action steps to stop the slide into burnout and have support in doing so.

Keeping your red flags in front of you will help you recognize more quickly when you're in the danger zone, and there is no shame in asking for help.

You may find that, over time, those red-flag zones change, or the ways you address them need to be updated. What's crucial here is that you know what baseline and burnout look like for you, the danger zone in between, and how to correct course when you're in that zone.

Business owners will inevitably face burnout, but this system to handle red flags can prevent a lot of it.

CHAPTER TAKEAWAYS

Burnout red flags are repetitive actions, thoughts, and behaviors—they are internal to us. They are also measurable. While external forces may affect them, we ultimately have a great deal of control over our red flags.

- To identify your red flags, look to past stressful times in your life.
- Most business owners don't go from "everything is great" to burnout overnight. It is essential for you to know what your "normal" or baseline is for each red flag, as well as your burnout level. The space in between those two markers is your danger zone.
- If you're in your danger zone, you have the opportunity to stop the slide from baseline to burnout by addressing each red flag with actions you identified in this chapter. Having an awareness of these red flags at all times is crucial to recognizing them early on so that you can correct course.
- You can choose accountability partners to help you maintain this awareness—remember, there's no shame in asking for help.

CHAPTER 3

Burnout Triggers

Burnout triggers differ from red flags because triggers are external to you. They tend to be other people, places, or situations. They show up at work as well as in your personal life. For example, I know a lot of business owners with a family member who is a burnout trigger.

Triggers also tend to cause you immediate stress. For some, just the thought of a trigger will raise their stress level. If someone has repeated exposure to a trigger, or even repeated thoughts of being around that trigger, that ongoing, never-ending stress can lead to burnout.

There's a reason why some people use the word *dread* to describe going to work every morning. Work is a trigger for them that causes immense stress before they even get there.

In this chapter, you'll identify your triggers and create a plan for how you'll deal with them. The bad news about triggers is that you can't control what someone or something else does. The good news about triggers is that you can control how you interact with and react to them.

Chapter Overview

Section	Summary
Step 1: Identify Your Triggers	A definition of burnout triggers, plus some common examples and a guide to identifying a few of your own.
Step 2: Categorize Your Triggers	How to separate your triggers into three categories to help you determine which ones you can eliminate.
Step 3: Plan for Triggers You Can't Eliminate	How to interact with triggers you will continue to face.

STEP 1: IDENTIFY YOUR TRIGGERS

Are there two or three people, places, and/or situations that are causing you unbearable stress right now? If not right now, how about in the past? These are your triggers—select two or three of them and write them down.

To get you started, here are some triggers I've heard about over the years from business owners:

A parent's Alzheimer's diagnosis	The phone ringing
Having a baby	The weekend
An employee passing away	A particular feeling on certain days of the week

A family member passing away	The feeling of sitting in one's office chair
An upcoming vacation	Working from home
Threats from disgruntled employees or clients	A smartphone ping signaling a new text or email
The news	A TV or music turned on or off
A coworker's voice, perfume, or simply the coworker themselves	A spouse's bad mood
Buying software	The holidays
Unexpected growth at one's company	A favorite doctor's unexpected retirement

The examples go on and on.

Sometimes seemingly small but recurring triggers that go undefined as such can cause burnout. Don't judge yourself here—you are the only one who will see your list.

Recognizing Crossover Between Red Flags and Triggers

At times, triggers can cause red flags to show up. For example, needing to fire an employee at work is a trigger for most business owners. It's a trigger because it's external—it's about an employee (another person) at work (an external place). However, the stress of that trigger can cause some of a person's red flags to show up. A person in this situation might not sleep well during this time or might not want to hang out with friends.

There is crossover between red flags and triggers, but there is also a line between the two. When a trigger is dealt with, those red flags that the trigger activated will often return to baseline on their own. If they don't, you can go back to your plan of how to turn a red flag around and get back to baseline yourself.

STEP 2: CATEGORIZE YOUR TRIGGERS

You're now going to separate the burnout triggers you've just identified into three categories: "can eliminate," "can limit/avoid," and "cannot limit/avoid." You'll then create a plan for dealing with the triggers you can't eliminate.

Triggers You Can Eliminate

Notifications on your phone may be a trigger you could eliminate. A blaring TV, overconsumption of social media, a certain office at work, a networking group you attend regularly—these are all items you can eliminate. If you can eliminate a trigger, do it.

Triggers You Can Limit

Limiting exposure to a trigger may put you at ease and will lessen its impact on you. You'll still have to face the trigger, but if you can limit your exposure to it, that's a great step.

Examples of burnout triggers you can limit exposure to may include a client at work whose emails stress you out before you even open them or those phone calls that you must make during "regular business hours" on behalf of your elderly parents and/or children. We'll cover possible solutions to limit your exposure to these triggers in step three of this process.

Triggers You Cannot Limit

Ideally, we could eliminate or limit exposure to all our burnout triggers, but sometimes that isn't possible. Examples of triggers that are challenging (or impossible) to eliminate or limit include a new baby, a parent or friend with a terminal illness, and a project at work that stresses you out but provides immense benefit to your company. These are triggers that we cannot, or do not want to, eliminate or limit—but they are triggers nonetheless.

STEP 3: PLAN FOR TRIGGERS YOU CAN'T ELIMINATE

Triggers You Can Limit

For triggers in this category, make a plan for how you will limit your exposure and then implement it. Limiting exposure to triggers usually involves a mix of setting boundaries and utilizing technology.

For example, what about the client emails that stress you out before you even open them? Here are some options to help you limit the stress of that trigger:

- Filter the client's emails into a separate inbox and look at that folder only three times per week.
- Set up an autoresponder stating that you have a one- to two-business-day turnaround on email responses.
- Have a conversation with the client about their email practices and request fewer emails so that you can better serve them.
- Set up a monthly or quarterly meeting with the client to "facilitate better communication between us and reduce email correspondence."

For those phone calls you must make on behalf of a family member during regular business hours, here are a few options that could help limit exposure to the burnout trigger:

- Schedule making those phone calls during your least productive work time. For me, that's on Thursdays and Fridays between 1 PM and 3 PM (the afternoon slump).
- The next time you make a call, ask if there's an option for correspondence through an online portal or a direct email.
- Ask for help from others who play a part in caregiving. For example, if you have a co-parent, ask them to make some of the phone calls.

Sometimes we get stuck in a loop of doing things the same way we've always done them, not realizing there are other options. Looking for ways to limit your exposure to burnout triggers requires you to be resourceful and consider other options.

But hey—you're a business owner. You *are* resourceful. It's time to use that resourcefulness to identify a plan to help you limit exposure to triggers.

Triggers You Cannot Limit or Avoid

Acceptance is the first step in dealing with burnout triggers you cannot limit. I have seen and experienced that, sometimes, acknowledging this fact helps reduce the stress around it.

For example, instead of thinking, "I hate this project at work; it causes me so much stress," you could reframe that as, "This project at work is a burnout trigger for me, but it provides a lot of value to my company."

The second step in dealing with the triggers you cannot limit is to set boundaries for how you react to them. Remember—you may not be able to control the trigger, but you can control your reaction. For example, thinking, "I hate this project at work," and letting that thought end there might lead to procrastination. What if you take that a bit further when you're faced with this burnout trigger? For example, you could change your reaction from the above to, "I hate this project at work, so I'll complete it as soon as I get to work. That way, I won't have to think about it again for a while." Choosing immediate action instead of waiting until later to address the project is one way to control your reaction to a burnout trigger.

Third, reward yourself for facing the burnout trigger. Continuing to use that work project as an example, perhaps you could set aside part of the revenue from that project for a dream vacation or an item you've wanted to buy for a very long time.

You could also plan breaks from that project. For example, you work on the project for four weeks, and then you get a one-week break. Then you do another cycle of four weeks on, one week off.

There are hundreds of examples, but what is most important is the work you do to identify your own burnout triggers, accept that you can't limit some of them, and then find a way to manage your own expectations and reactions to them.

Additional Guidance for Triggers You Cannot Limit

While there is no one-size-fits-all approach for dealing with unavoidable triggers, I find that it's helpful to have a place to start. Working with these burnout triggers you cannot limit is about knowing what is in your control and what is not.

If It's a People Trigger . . .

Change your own behavior and set firm boundaries—it's okay to say no to some interactions. It's also okay to tell someone you will not discuss certain topics with them. Look for ways to enjoy the person and try to put away the parts that trigger you. Always remember that it's okay to cut a visit short if needed.

If It's a Place Trigger . . .

Adopt and plan a new routine when you must go to the place, and then do not deviate from that plan. Set a time limit for how much time you will spend in that place.

Part of your new routine may include a reward for going to the place and for when you leave that place. Try to reward yourself with something healthy—extra sleep before going and hanging out with friends after you leave. While you're at that place, you can do things like listen to music, take a break to meditate, or take a walk several times a day for ten minutes.

When your time limit is up, leave.

If It's a Situation Trigger . . .

Before you find yourself in the situation, try to identify one positive aspect of it. It may be that you're looking forward to eating at a new restaurant in which the situation trigger will occur.

Using scripts and having a few general one-liners will help you get through some situation burnout triggers. For example, in just about any situation, it's fine to say, "Please excuse me," and then get up and walk away from it for a few minutes. If you're worried about going to a new business networking group and consider that a situation trigger, practicing your "elevator pitch" in advance can help a lot.

Taking a buffer with you to some situations may also help. That buffer could be a pet, a friend, an employee, or an object to share—something that breaks the ice in the given situation. Whatever will make you feel more at ease. The key here is to have something planned.

Summary Table

When you can't limit a . . .	You can . . .
People trigger	Change your own behavior and set firm boundaries. Refuse to discuss certain topics and cut visits short if needed.
Place trigger	Plan a new routine for when you must go to the place. Reward yourself with something healthy before and after the visit.
Situation trigger	Use a script or have some one-liners ready, excuse yourself from the situation for a few minutes, and consider a buffer.

With any kind of trigger, the first thing to remember is that it is your job to take care of yourself. For triggers you cannot eliminate, the best way to take care of yourself is with a plan that includes boundaries.

I recognize that planning and then implementing your response to burnout triggers may be very hard. However, the goal here is to prevent burnout; sometimes that requires hard work. Part of that hard work is maintaining your awareness about both red flags and triggers in your daily life.

CHAPTER TAKEAWAYS

Burnout triggers are external to the business owner: other people, places, and situations. These triggers increase stress levels, which can lead to burnout.

- Entrepreneurs cannot control burnout triggers, but they can control how they interact with and react to those triggers.
- Founders can sort their triggers into three categories: "can eliminate," "can limit/avoid," and "cannot limit/avoid." Business owners can create a plan for how they will interact with each trigger they cannot eliminate.
- The key to dealing with burnout triggers is recognizing what you can control instead of trying to control the triggers themselves.

Part II

BATTLING
BURNOUT

CHAPTER 4

Make Space to
Address Burnout

When you are a business owner acknowledging burnout, there's often a moment of panic. You look at your schedule, your workload, your life, and wonder, "How can I make space to deal with my burnout while also running a business and having a personal life?"

The worry you may feel comes from two directions. First, you know you need to address the burnout because, no matter the cause, it's not sustainable for your business or for you, so there's a sense of urgency. Second, you have no idea where you will make space to address your burnout.

The term "make space" can mean a lot of things. It is most often a reallocation of existing resources. Time, energy, money, and physical space—all of us have some limits around each of these resources.

You yourself are a limited resource; remembering this will help you determine how you go through this part of the process.

Making space can take many forms. It can mean creating space on your calendar. It can also mean going to a specific physical location (your backyard, a conference room, your favorite coffee shop) where you can address your burnout. Remember to consider your energy levels when making space—your energy level at 8 AM on a Monday morning is completely different than at 4 PM on a Thursday afternoon.

You may find yourself feeling overwhelmed at this point. That's normal. I've got you. You will find some space—it just requires looking at things a little differently. Here's a mini road map for this chapter to put you at ease.

Chapter Overview

Section	Summary
Who Said You *Have* to Slow Down?	A reframing of the idea that you must slow down to make space.
Step 1: Say No to New Step 2: Determine Which Business Initiatives Can Be Paused	Steps to determine which bigger-picture initiatives you can decline or pause right now to create space.
Step 3: What You Do on a Regular Basis	A step to write down all the tasks in your business and personal life that you do on a recurring basis, in order to make space for burnout.
Step 4: What Tasks Can You Eliminate? Step 5: What Tasks Can You Delegate? Step 6: Identify Tasks You Can Do Later	Steps to help you eliminate, delegate, and postpone the tasks on your current to-do list.
Step 7: Prioritize Your To-Do List Step 8: Implement Your Plan	A framework, some insightful questions, and guidance to help you prioritize your remaining tasks and implement an effective plan.

As you read through this chapter and complete the work, you may wonder how much space you need to create. That'll depend on what you discovered in chapter two. The number of burnout red flags you currently exhibit, and where you are in your danger zones, will dictate how much room to create. The more red flags you exhibit and the closer you are to burnout in your danger zones, the more space you'll need.

Once you make this space, you'll use it to address, recover from, and leverage burnout. I go into more detail about each of those steps in upcoming chapters.

In this chapter, you'll learn how to make space to address burnout without slowing down, taking a long break, or a going on a vacation. You'll learn a process and be given practical tools for making space. The rest of this book is built on the assumption that you have done this work. There's no one-size-fits-all directive to making space, but there is a process you can follow to help you find the answers that are right for you and your business. This chapter builds the foundation to enable business owners to continue working while addressing burnout.

A Note on Vacations and Breaks (aka Escapes)

Sometimes a vacation is part of the solution. I stress the words "part of" because a vacation alone doesn't fix the stress that awaits your return.

Travis Rosbach, founder of the Tumalo Group and Hydro Flask, is a serial entrepreneur. He loves business and is currently an advisor to other business owners. But even he, someone who by all standard definitions of business-owner success has "made it," has dealt with burnout.

Before Hydro Flask, Travis owned a fencing company, and this is where he experienced business-owner burnout for the first time. Travis says, "I had worked about eighteen months straight without a break. We got our first time-card punch machine because we needed a better system to manage employee time sheets." But his employees noticed that Travis wasn't clocking in and out. His initial reaction was that he didn't need to do so because he was the owner. But to be fair, he started clocking his hours. Travis reminded himself, "It's Seal Team 6, not Seal Team 5 + 1. A leader is still part of the team." After one week, Travis was surprised by what he saw.

"I had worked eighty-eight hours in that week. It was cold—it was February. I was out there digging holes in the ice and snow, and my fingers weren't working anymore. I was sore. It was awful. I knew then I was burned out."

Like many business owners, Travis thought a vacation was the answer to his burnout. The vacation he took helped, but upon return, Travis decided to sell the fencing company. "I got burned out, and I sold. What I learned, though, is that it's very smart to have a game plan for that. I now think it's important for business owners to have some sort of exit strategy when they start a business."

This is a great example of why taking a vacation is often not the solution. A vacation may help the burnout-recovery journey, but it's usually not the first or the last step. It never solves all the underlying problems. This chapter is not about escaping burnout; it's about making space for you to resolve it.

WHO SAID YOU *HAVE* TO SLOW DOWN?

The most common question I hear from business owners when it comes to this part of the work is, "How do I slow down enough to make space?" This part of the process, it turns out, doesn't necessarily require you to slow down. In fact, making this room often propels your business more quickly toward your goals.

This exercise is about reprioritizing and honoring your well-being. Does it sometimes mean you'll have to slow down? Yes. But I've also seen (and experienced myself) that once a CEO does make space for burnout, they are much more productive and seem to move at a faster pace than before. Here's a little secret: making space creates a more sustainable and better-prioritized pace of work and life.

Some business owners time-block on their calendars. Some learn to accommodate their energy levels throughout the day and week. Some look for alternative physical work locations (such as coffee shops, conference rooms, or kitchen tables) that are separate from their normal workplace. Some find room in their bank accounts by investing in resources that help them make space.

You don't have to slow down to make space for burnout, but you do need to reprioritize. Here's the process to do so.

STEP 1: NO TO NEW*

Most business owners love a new opportunity—a shiny new idea to work on. But when you're addressing burnout, it's not the time to chase those opportunities. Saying no to those new ideas is an important first step toward addressing the never-ending stress that's gotten you here.

Say no to anything new* during this time—even if it seems like the most awesome opportunity in the world. It isn't. Another will come. It's not the right time, and the resources you would have put into that new idea can now go toward making space.

*With one exception: the new process you're learning in this book.

No to New Protects You

Travis Rosbach makes space by being very protective of his privacy and time. "When I sold Hydro Flask, people started coming out of the woodwork—asking for money and time. I didn't anticipate this and was scammed. Today, though, I'm very picky about who I work with. I only say yes to clients who don't care who I was before—they just want results. I love diving into business without all the personal stuff." Travis has learned how to say no to new in many ways, which helps him make space to prevent and leverage burnout.

Also remember that this is not a no forever; it's no for now. I keep a Google Doc to store the new ideas and opportunities that show up, and I'll revisit that list later, at a better time. By using technology to make a space for these ideas, I don't worry about forgetting them. This also frees up my mind to do this burnout-recovery work (without a hundred new ideas taking up space in there).

This no to new, for now, should be in both your business life and your personal life. The space you make in this part of the plan is earmarked for later work to help you address, recover from, prevent, and leverage burnout.

STEP 2: DETERMINE WHICH BUSINESS INITIATIVES CAN BE PAUSED

The next step in making space is to review business initiatives you've said yes to and determine which of those can be paused. This does not include the day-to-day operations of your business—for example, business development, customer service, payroll, and all the other daily operations, which should continue.

This step reviews the bigger-picture initiatives and projects to figure out which of them can be put on hold for now—and not forever. Here's how to work through this step.

Create a List of All Business Initiatives

To determine which initiatives to pause, you first need a list of the current ones.

You're going to prioritize and pause business initiatives first before working on your to-do list. You'll look at these larger projects first because the work associated with each project you pause will no longer be on your to-do list. This step helps you reduce your daily task list before you even review it!

Examples of business initiatives may include creating and launching a new product or service, finding a new bookkeeper or financial advisor, transitioning to a new software everyone uses at the company, moving offices, working with your attorney to rewrite your contracts, or launching a full rebrand of the company.

If you're unclear as to what should be listed here, it's really any business initiative that is outside the day-to-day operations.

Determine What to Pause

Are those examples I just mentioned important initiatives? Yes. Does your company already have a structure in place to get those jobs done? Most likely, yes. Can some of those initiatives be paused so that you can make space? Again, most likely, yes.

Deciding which initiatives to pause will be based on many variables, so there's no cut-and-dried "pause this, not that" guide. However, there are a few questions that can guide you in identifying what projects can wait.

Questions to Guide You	Examples and Considerations
How close is the finish line?	If an initiative is 80 percent complete, it may be worth finishing. If an initiative just started, it may be ideal to pause.
Are contracts involved that you cannot pause?	If your company just signed a new contract for a yearlong project, it may be difficult to put it on hold. But even if the contract has specific timelines, you can still ask if any pause is possible.
Will pausing the initiative do great harm to your company?	If you've just discovered that your CPA made a big mistake on your tax returns and you need to find a new service provider, that's a good initiative to move forward on. Pausing this project may negatively affect your finances.
Is the opportunity you've already decided to pursue worth it? Will it still exist in six months?	If you have a great opportunity that may pass you by, it could be worth moving forward. These are questions to consider carefully, however, because it's easy to get excited by opportunities.

For business owners, deciding which initiatives to pause is often the most difficult step in making space to address burnout because these big-picture projects are often what we enjoy the most. However, discerning between the ones that can be paused and the ones that need to continue is a key part of the plan. Every business is different, and the projects that can be paused for one business won't be the same for another. It depends on industry, company size, goals, timing, and many other variables.

At this point, you will have a list of business initiatives that your company will pause. Now we'll get into your day-to-day to-do list.

STEP 3: WHAT YOU DO ON A REGULAR BASIS

Now comes the part where you write down tasks you do on a recurring basis. Note your tasks from both work and your personal life. To make space for burnout, you want to look at everything.

You'll want to note any existing self-care activities you do. These so often get pushed to the back of our minds when we think of our to-do list, but if you're regularly doing them, write them down. Some common personal-life items I've seen business owners write down here include exercising, spending time with friends and family, meditating, managing finances, reading, and doing chores.

As you make this list, it may be helpful to note how frequently you do each task (daily, weekly, monthly, quarterly, etc.), but that isn't required.

This list will only include tasks and activities you already do. This isn't a list of things you try or want to do but don't. For example, if you already make dinner three times a week, that goes on the list. If you *want* to make dinner, but you do not already participate in the process, then making dinner does not go on the list. We'll cover your wants in the prevention plan in chapter nine.

I am often asked questions like, "Should I include sleeping, eating, or taking showers in this list?" For me, I've found that listing individual items that fall under a larger category clutters my list. Instead, I'll write down "Get ready for bed," for example, which means about an hour and a half to clean up the kitchen from dinner, read or do something else to unwind, take a shower, and turn off the lights. However, if you feel it's important to add all the separate tasks to your list, add them.

STEP 4: WHAT TASKS CAN YOU ELIMINATE?

Now that you have your list of tasks you do on a regular basis, it's time to sort it into four categories. These categories will help you determine what *you* must continue to do even while addressing and recovering from your burnout. It will also help you identify what actions can come off your plate to make space.

The four categories are "eliminate," "delegate," "later," and "do." You will triage your list into these four categories in the next several steps; you will then put that triaging into motion after you do this initial sorting of your list.

Eliminating items on your list is the first step because if you can cross them off your to-do list, that creates space that doesn't require much else from you. You may need to have a conversation with another party, but that's often all you need to do.

Here are some questions to help you decide what to eliminate from your list. As you go through these questions, remember that delegating and doing something later are both options as well.

Is There Any Value for the Business or for You in That Task?

Value can be defined in many ways. Money, peace of mind, growth, health, and time are all valuable. If there is a task on your to-do list that currently provides no value to you or your business, eliminate it.

It's okay to eliminate actions you once found valuable but no longer do. Likewise, actions that may be valuable in the future but are not currently valuable to you can be eliminated. Here are two examples I've experienced, one in business and one in my personal life.

At one point, being a member of a few business networking organizations was a crucial part of my business growth. Over the years, the value of those memberships has declined (they are still valuable to others, just not to me right now). I discontinued my memberships, which saved money and time—making space for other things, like preventing and leveraging burnout.

I've also eliminated affirmations from my morning routine. I used to have around five statements I'd say out loud every morning in my backyard. For many years, that practice improved my self-confidence and got me ready for the day. The last six months I engaged in this practice, though, I didn't feel like it was of value to me or my business. Even though it had been very valuable in the past, it was no longer helpful, so I stopped the practice.

As we go through business and life, priorities change. What was once a crucial part of your workday or your life at home may no longer be important. Habits are great, but when we get burned out and need to make space, it is worth reviewing even those long-standing practices.

Can Someone Else Determine If the Task Is of Value, or Is the Task Something You Can Reexamine Later?

"I don't know" is an acceptable answer to the first question about value, even when you're evaluating your own to-do list. If you don't know, someone else may be able to answer the value question for you. Or you may need to wait for valuation. If you don't know a task's value, that task then becomes "Evaluate the value of [task]" and is moved to either the "delegate" or "later" list. Either way, you've eliminated it from your current to-do list.

After asking these two questions, you'll most likely have eliminated some tasks, identified others to delegate for evaluation, or put some things on your "later" list. Hopefully you've now made some space to address and recover from burnout.

But we're not done yet—let's keep going with your list.

STEP 5: WHAT TASKS CAN YOU DELEGATE?

After you make your first pass through the list and figure out what to eliminate, the next step is identifying tasks to delegate. Any task that goes into the "delegate" category will have a corresponding item on your to-do list to hand it off to another team member. Creating or updating a process, teaching the team member, and checking their work (at first) are examples of corresponding tasks on your to-do list that go along with delegating. If you already have someone to delegate these tasks to, great! If not, you'll have a bit more work to do to find someone to whom you can delegate. This doesn't mean you have to be the one to find the help (you can delegate this!). This also doesn't mean you must hire an employee; often, you can hire a subcontractor or another company to help you with these items.

While there are a few extra tasks to do initially, delegating can be one of the best ways to make space because tasks will still get completed, just not by you. When you're looking for tasks on your list to delegate, there are a few questions to ask.

Are You the Best Person for the Task?

You have a specific set of skills that make you highly valuable to your company, to your team at work, and in your personal life. As you look at the tasks on your list, ask yourself if you are the best person for those tasks. If a task is something someone else can do better than you can (or even 80 percent as well as you can), consider it for delegation. The rest of the questions in this section will help you determine which category that task belongs in, but for now, mark it as a possible delegation.

Avoid Micromanaged Misery

Meghan Lynch is all about nurturing a positive and strong workplace culture. There was a time, though, when Meghan had created a culture that she didn't even want to work in—which led to her burnout.

Meghan shares, "There was a point in the company where I was not able to delegate. I would give people things and then immediately take them back or undermine them. I only realized afterward that I was creating this culture of mistrust or lack of safety. People didn't feel safe to fail because if they did, I was going to swoop in and take something back or undermine them in front of the client."

Meghan realized that she had created an atmosphere of fear, one with a lot of back-channel chatter and mistrust. A workplace that even she, the owner, didn't want to be a part of. She says, "I thought that if I'm going to own a business, I want to own a business I want to go to work in."

Meghan got to work on building an atmosphere of trust and mutual respect.

Foster Trust

It's often hard for business owners to trust others with their companies. The more important the work is to the company, the harder it is for entrepreneurs to let go. The key to avoiding micromanaged misery is to set clear expectations of outcomes for the person to whom the work is delegated.

It's also important to set up parameters for expected failure—that's what protects the founder from swooping in to "save" the work. If you set up some guardrails within which a person can fail but still successfully meet or exceed your expectations, you'll be less likely to try to rescue the project because you'll know they can't drive the car (in this case, your business) off the cliff. Guardrails can be time, budget, milestones, skill level, and a variety of other elements that prevent a project from heading over the edge into a ravine.

Is This Task Something That Must Be Done Now or Soon?

If the answer is no, this task can go into the "later" category. Even if you can delegate it, if it doesn't need to be done now or soon, do it later. Remember, this is temporary. Eventually, that "later" category will be addressed. Right now, though, you're making as much space as possible for burnout.

If the answer to this question is yes—this task must be done now or soon—then you go to the next question.

Is There Someone Else Who Already Works for Your Business or Is Already in Your Personal Life Who Could Do This Task?

If the answer is yes, the task goes into the "delegate" category, with a note about whom you will delegate the task to.

On this question, I want to emphasize the "already works for / in your life" part. Hiring new employees or contractors takes up a lot of space for most business owners, so first determine if your existing team (both at work and at home) can take on the tasks you need to delegate. If you find that you do need to add new team members at this point, I highly encourage you to delegate as much of the recruiting and hiring process as possible to your existing team.

For example, let's say you need to hire a salesperson. Reviewing résumés, interviewing, checking references, onboarding, training, and all the other tasks that go into hiring take a lot of time (and energy). What parts of the process can your existing team tackle? Could you bring on an HR consultant or recruiter to help? As the business owner, you can (and should) be involved in the hiring process, but you don't have to do it all by yourself.

On the personal side, let's say one of your tasks is to get someone to fix a plumbing issue (or something similar) at home. Finding the right plumber could take an incredible amount of effort—between sorting through calendars, determining the nature and urgency of the problem, and deciphering online reviews, you'll have a lot of work on your hands! Could you ask your partner or a family member for help in part (or all) of that process?

This point is so important that I'll say it once more: If you need to add new team members, delegate as much of this piece of the delegation process as possible.

Fortunately, you have a support network to ask for help.

Who and How to Ask for Help

First, you must identify the people in your support network whom you will ask for help. At work, a business partner, a key employee, or your leadership team would be ideal people to ask about delegation. And even if they can't take over the task for now, they may be able to help find someone who can.

In your personal life, a significant other is often the first choice. You could also ask a best friend or a family member. Those individuals may be able to help you by taking some of the items off your to-do list.

Once you identify who you'll ask for help, you ask them. If it feels uncomfortable to be that direct, providing more context about the expectations can make it easier to ask.

For example, a direct ask to an employee sounds like this: "We need a salesperson and I'd like you to lead the hiring process. Will you manage this initiative?"

A context-filled ask sounds like this: "We need to hire a salesperson for the company. I trust your judgment, and I'd like you to take on the project of hiring and onboarding. I expect it to take four months from start to finish; we can reprioritize your existing tasks to give you the time to do this. I'll be in on the final interviews, final selection, and welcoming the new hire during their first two weeks, but other than that, I'd like you to manage this initiative."

While the version with more context may seem wordy, remember this is about making it easier for you to ask for help. Whatever gets you over the hurdle of asking—do it!

If the people you ask say yes to your request for help, share the list of possible tasks for delegating. You may wish to share your entire list with them, or you can narrow it down to tasks that are only relevant to their role, responsibilities, and strengths. When you share the list, schedule a meeting for a few days later to agree on a plan of action.

Based on these questions, you now likely have less on your to-do list and much more in the "eliminate" and "delegate" categories. Now we'll tackle what's left to get some clarity on your remaining list.

STEP 6: IDENTIFY TASKS YOU CAN DO LATER

At this point, you're probably realizing you've done an activity like this before. Most business owners have. But what's often missing in those activities is a "later" category.

Sometimes our tasks aren't as cut-and-dried as "eliminate," "delegate," or "do." Sometimes we know a task can wait until later. Often, we don't know the answer to the questions above. The lack of this additional category hinders a business owner's ability to make space because such tasks usually end up staying on their to-do list with nowhere else to go.

Let's agree here that some tasks can wait and some tasks you won't be sure how to categorize. Those tasks belong in the "later" category, and here are some questions that can help you identify them.

Will Your Doing or Not Doing This Task Make a Big Difference a Year from Now?

You already determined this task had value in the "eliminate" step. You also determined you cannot delegate this task. There is a reason the task in question has made it to this step, and it often has to do with uncertainty regarding long-term impact.

If the answer to this question is yes, the task stays on your to-do list. If the answer is no, eliminate doing it for now (it may be something you do later). If you're still on the fence about it, it belongs in the "later" category.

For example, if those networking groups were still on my list but I got to this step and decided that discontinuing them would not make a big difference for me in a year, then I would know to eliminate that task. If I wasn't sure, I'd put it into the "later" category.

That leaky faucet, though? That could be a big (costly and not covered by home insurance) problem in a year. If I don't already have someone to help me find a plumber, that task would stay on my to-do list.

I have seen entrepreneurs eliminate marketing, events, meetings, and existing services or products here. I've seen others decide to keep those items on their to-do list, and I've seen still others put those same items into the "later" category.

The answer to this question will greatly depend on your business and what you've already discovered while making space.

What Does Your Gut Instinct Say?

It's nice to have all the facts and figures we need to make a decision. But often we don't have all the information we would like. When that's the case, a big part of our decision-making comes down to our gut instincts. That rule applies here.

When you have a task that you can't determine if you should keep on your to-do list or put in the "later" category, what does your gut instinct say?

There is a lot of educated guessing in business ownership. One lesson I've learned, though, is that if my gut is telling me something, I'd better listen to it. This is a good time to put that lesson into practice.

If your gut instinct doesn't give you a clear direction at this point, put the task in question in the "later" category. If your gut says the task is a keeper, keep it on your to-do list. Even if it's a task that others have advised you to delegate or stop doing, keep doing it.

Your gut instinct is rarely wrong; when you're in doubt, listen to it.

Every task you've categorized up to this point has created space—congratulations! You've decided to eliminate or delegate tasks. You've also made some space by putting some tasks in the "later" category.

Summary Table

To help you determine if you can . . .	Ask yourself these questions:
Eliminate a task.	Is there any value for the business or for you in that task? Can someone else determine if the task is worth your time?
Delegate a task.	Are you the best person for the task? Is it something that must be done now or soon? Is there someone else who already works for your business or is already in your personal life who could do this task?

To help you determine if you can . . .	Ask yourself these questions:
Do a task later.	Will your doing or not doing the task now make a big difference a year from now? What does your gut instinct say?

Now it's time to take stock of what's still on your to-do list and tackle prioritization.

STEP 7: PRIORITIZE YOUR TO-DO LIST

I saved your to-do list for last because I want you to have as little remaining on it as possible. Going through the other three categories first helped you eliminate, delegate, and determine what to do later.

Doing the steps in this order ensures your remaining to-do list isn't as daunting to prioritize. Because you've created some space, this part of the process is a little easier, since there are fewer tasks left to review. At this point, the tasks remaining on your list will likely stay on your to-do list.

Some common work-related items I've seen business owners keep on their to-do list while they're dealing with burnout include business development/sales, leadership, client-relationship management for large clients, and already-planned strategic initiatives that they had decided would continue.

What stays on your to-do list will greatly depend on your life and your resources. For example, many chores and household-maintenance items can be outsourced, but if you don't have the budget to hire someone to mow your lawn or don't have another family member that can take it off your list, those tasks will have to stay.

What we're going to do in this step is prioritize the tasks remaining on your to-do list. Here are a few questions that can help you prioritize your remaining tasks.

Is There a Deadline and/or Consequence Associated with This Task?

If the answer to this is yes, the task moves to a higher priority on your to-do list. If the answer is no, the task can be moved to the bottom of your to-do list. Addressing, recovering from, and preventing future burnout, for example, may not have a deadline, but neglecting to do so could have dire consequences—so that work stays on your to-do list and should be near the top of it.

How Close Is the Deadline, and/or How Severe Is the Consequence?

To sort the items that had a yes answer to the first question, the next question is about timeline. If you have a deadline one month away and a deadline six months away, the work related to the deadline that's one month away takes priority.

Also prioritize based on the severity of potential consequences. If you have a task on your to-do list that could have severe consequences if not completed, that is a high priority. Other tasks may have consequences if neglected, but they might be tolerable. The severity of consequences is subjective and will depend on your specific situation.

The closer a deadline is, and/or the more severe the potential consequences of not doing the work are, the higher that task goes on your prioritized to-do list.

Does the Task Energize or Drain You?

After sorting based on deadline and/or consequences, ask yourself if the task in question gives you energy or drains you.

A task that gives you energy but has not yet been prioritized goes higher on the to-do list. Tasks without deadlines or consequences that drain you go at the very bottom of the to-do list.

You Have Your Newly Prioritized, Much Shorter To-Do List!

The goal of these list-sorting steps is to cut as much out as possible so that you can address your burnout more effectively. For tasks that must remain on your to-do list, the goal of the steps above was to help you prioritize them.

Now that you have a grasp on what is still on your to-do list *and* the order in which to approach those tasks, I suggest you take a short break of two or three days before moving on to the next step. Stepping away from challenging work gives us a fresh perspective when we return.

STEP 8: IMPLEMENT YOUR PLAN

After your short break, take a quick look at your remaining to-do list and see if your decisions about anything on it have changed. If so, make those changes. Then you get to eliminate and delegate tasks as planned.

Eliminating tasks is straightforward. It might require an uncomfortable conversation and a few other transition items, but once it's done, it's done.

Delegating, on the other hand, can be a challenge. It doesn't happen overnight, and there are many great books written on the art of delegation. When it comes to delegating, I have four pieces of advice:

- **Make sure the person to whom you are delegating a task knows the quality expectation.** To set someone up for success, they must know how success will be defined. It is your job as a leader to make sure the person you delegate to understands the quality expectations. Process documents can help communicate expectations.
- **No one will do the work the same way you do, even if you have an existing process.** Accept this when going into delegation. Others may do it better than you. They may do it differently than you. What matters is that they do the work at a level of established quality standards.
- **Verify and teach.** Verify that the work is being done up to the quality standards. If it's not, teach the person how to elevate to those standards.
- **Trust your gut.** First, trust your gut about the person to whom you've chosen to delegate a task. Then trust your gut about the work they are doing. If something seems off in either of those elements, it probably is. Review it and course-correct.

If you do this repeatedly, over time you'll find yourself getting better at delegating. You'll have fewer delegated tasks that end up back on your plate.

Once you've worked through the delegated items, take a deep breath. You've just done quite a bit of work on your to-do list.

YOU'VE MADE SPACE FOR BURNOUT!

It wasn't easy. I'm sure some difficult decisions were made. You started with one list of everything you do regularly and analyzed it in detail. You eliminated and delegated tasks. Your remaining to-do list is more manageable because you've prioritized the tasks on it, which may give you more energy because you now don't have to decide which task to start with every day.

You've made space in many ways—appreciate it! You've done important and challenging work here. Notice just how much room you've created—whether that's time, energy, money, or a sense of relief.

Now that you've made space, you're ready to use that space to face your burnout head-on. The next few chapters will walk you through the steps to battle burnout.

CHAPTER TAKEAWAYS

- To address and recover from burnout, business owners will need to make some space. It's not just about time—it could include budget, energy levels, or physical space for certain work.
- Saying no to new is a crucial part of making space for burnout. It is important for self-made CEOs to understand that this no-to-new mentality could be only a no for now. You can always decide to try

something later on, just not while you are making
space for burnout.

- Sorting your current to-do list into four categories—
  "eliminate," "delegate," "later," and "do"—is a
  process you can use to make space. Each category
  has specific questions to ask yourself that can help
  you determine which category a task falls within.

- The tasks that remain on your to-do list will need to be
  further prioritized. There are a few questions you can
  ask to help you prioritize your remaining list.

CHAPTER 5

Identify Burnout Types and Timelines

To get started, I think it's important to turn to an authorita-
tive source for a definition of burnout. The World Health Organization (WHO) defines burnout as follows:

> *Burnout is a syndrome conceptualized as resulting from chronic*
> *workplace stress that has not been successfully managed. It is charac-*
> *terized by three dimensions:*

> - *feelings of energy depletion or exhaustion*
> - *increased mental distance from one's job, or feelings of*
>   *negativism or cynicism related to one's job*
> - *reduced professional efficacy*

Burnout refers specifically to phenomena in the occupational context and should not be applied to describe experiences in other areas of life.[4]

I feel this definition misses a key element—that personal life events and circumstances can also cause burnout—but I'm not going to take that up with the WHO just yet.

There are many other possible definitions, but here's how I define what it feels like: burnout is when you have very little or no energy left to move forward and you cannot see an end in sight to being in this state.

While I can honor many definitions as an objective reference point, your burnout experiences will be unique to you. What causes burnout, how we experience it, and how we recover from it differ from one human to another. A goal of this book is to help you know what burnout looks like for you specifically.

In my work with business owners, I often find three types of burnout: attentional, emotional, and physical. These types often appear in that order (but not always). I've also found there are typically two timelines for burnout. There's acute burnout, which is brought on by something that happens suddenly and unexpectedly. There's also chronic burnout, which is the buildup of never-ending, overwhelming stress.

A friend and I were discussing his experience with burnout. He said a few things that really hit home for me, but one idea in particular needs to be addressed here.

If we're always busy (which most of us are), how do we know when we're burned out?

Great question—there are several ways to know.

In this chapter, I share five ways to help you determine if you're burned out: four indicators based on your own judgement, as well as an objective assessment you can take. Then we're going to dive into the three types of burnout, as well as the two timelines. By the end of this chapter, you'll know how to identify if you are burned out, and you'll also know your types.

Chapter Overview

Section	Summary
Am I Burned Out? Five Ways to Tell	Five ways to tell if you're beyond stressed.
Determine the Type of Burnout	A breakdown of the three types of burnout and some questions to help you determine if you're suffering from one, two, or all three types.
Understanding Burnout Timelines	A definition of the two timelines of burnout, plus how each can benefit you and your business.

AM I BURNED OUT? FIVE WAYS TO TELL

Whenever I talk with business owners, I often hear something along the lines of, "I'm stressed, but I'm not burned out." There's a defense mechanism that comes up for a lot of us, which I understand. Stress is accepted as normal, but burnout can feel like failure for some.

To fix burnout, we must first be aware, and then accept, that we are beyond stressed. There are several indicators an entrepreneur can observe about themselves to determine if they are, in fact, beyond stressed.

Think of these indicators like canaries in the coal mine—alerting you that there's a problem with the potential to explode. At least one of these has shown up in almost every burned-out business owner I've spoken with. Be honest with yourself to see if any of these are true for you.

The "I Miss You" Rule

The first indicator is the statement "I miss you." Is a friend or loved one saying, "I miss you" to you? Do you sometimes even miss your past self? If the answer is yes, you may be burned out.

When a founder is experiencing burnout, they often become a workaholic. They often try to do more to overcome challenges. At some point, they decide it's worth it to prioritize work over every-thing else. But now the founder, their team, their loved ones, and the people around them are feeling it.

People start telling the business owner they miss them or miss how things used to be.

In one of my own experiences, I put in sixteen-hour days, seven days a week, for about six months before I realized I was burned out. That was only because my wife said to me, "I really miss you. I miss us." As visionaries, we tend to put our heads down, grind it out, and get it done.

Those words of missing you, said by someone who loves you, will often stop you in your tracks.

I don't have a set number of hours a week that defines a business owner as a workaholic. In my personal experience, it's more about what is accomplished and my work–life harmony. What I do know is this: in most cases, workaholics have little to no time for their personal life. If your significant other or your friends—people you used to see on a regular basis—start telling you they miss you, that's a canary in a coal mine. Pay attention to it.

A Bad Case of the "Ins"

The second indicator of business-owner burnout is a bad case of the "ins": inaction and indifference. There are two statements that entrepreneurs say a lot in this state. One is "I don't know," which comes from the inability to decide, leading to inaction. The second is "I don't care," which is pure indifference.

"I Don't Know"

First off, it's okay to not know the answer to something as a business owner. But it's an indication of burnout if you say, "I don't know," and then there's no follow-up action. Being resourceful is second nature to most entrepreneurs. Not knowing the answer is not the warning sign here. Having no drive to find the answer is the potential indicator.

"I don't know" may also come from indecisiveness, which is often a precursor to inaction. When I'm experiencing inaction and indecision, I can't decide on things that used to involve easy decisions. This goes beyond decision fatigue; this is not knowing and not pursuing the answer, or not being able to decide at all.

"I Don't Care"

The "I don't care" statement also indicates burnout. In my experience, it takes a lot for me to get to the point where I say, "I don't care." Most business owners would agree. When a founder says, "I don't care" about something specific, it might simply mean, "I don't care how you accomplish this task." But when they say, "I don't care" a lot about their own business—that's when it's time to step back and address possible burnout.

This is indifference. One way I check myself is that when I say, "I don't care" about something in my business, I will ask myself, "Okay, then what *do* you care about?" I may or may not answer, but it's a good way to keep myself aware (and accountable) for my own stress.

If you're finding yourself saying, "I don't care" or, "I don't know" frequently, you may be dealing with burnout.

The "Two Weeks" Rule

The third way to help you identify if you're already burned out is to ask yourself, "What happens to my business and my team if I'm suddenly out of the office for two weeks?" If your answer to this is, "I can't be gone for two weeks," that's a possible sign of burnout.

Special Scenarios

It's important to note that, at times, when this indicator suggests you're burned out, it might be due only to a particular scenario. For example, in the first two years of a new business, it's a challenge to be away from work for two weeks. For established business owners, there are also times when they absolutely cannot be away from the business for a two-week period.

Those times might include when your company is launching a new product or service, or perhaps when it is involved in a merger or acquisition. Another example might be onboarding a new employee who is integral to your operations and with whom you will work closely. Maybe you're on the verge of closing a huge new client and you have an upcoming pitch to prepare.

These special scenarios have an end date. The product is launched, the new employee is onboarded, and the acquisition is completed. The exception to the "I can't take two weeks off right now" rule is when the business owner has an end to that busy period in sight.

Normal Operations

The "two weeks" indicator may help identify burnout when the daily, normal operations of an established business rely greatly on the business owner, so much so that the owner can't take two weeks off from work. Either no one else can take over in the short term or the owner can't shut down their operations for two weeks at any point without a negative impact on the business.

I define "established business" as a business that has been in operation for three or more years and has at least one person (other than the business owner) working in the business. That person could be an employee or a key subcontractor.

If you are the owner of an established business and you can't imagine stepping away from your business for two weeks, that's another canary in the coal mine. What if external circumstances force you to step out of your business temporarily? What if you suddenly have to drop everything? Unless you're in one of those special scenarios we talked about earlier, this is a great way to gauge how close you are to burnout.

If you can easily take a week off, you're probably not that close to burnout. If you can only take a day off? Pay attention to that answer.

The "I'm Busy" Rule

When someone asks you, "How are you doing?" examine how you answer that question. "I'm busy" and "I have a lot going on" have become standard answers.

Carefully consider how you want to answer this question.

We're all busy. I used to answer "How are you doing?" with "I'm busy," too. But then I became more intentional in how I answer that question. If I'm overwhelmed, I say, "I'm overwhelmed," when someone asks me how I'm doing. If I'm in a good place, I say, "I'm doing well."

Sometimes "overwhelmed" and "busy" do not indicate burnout. What's more important here is your tone and how you truly want to answer the question.

How you respond to this kind of question can often be a mirror that shows you where you really are. The person who asks you this question might not be someone to whom you want to respond, "I'm really freaking stressed right now"—it's okay to tell someone you don't know, "I'm busy." But if you know the real answer is, "I'm overwhelmed, stressed, and tired," that may be a burnout indicator for you. Become aware of how you really *want* to answer the question "How are you?" and tune in to what you know is the truthful answer (even if you don't say it).

If you're honest with yourself, reviewing these indicators will help you identify if you're burned out. There's one other objective tool you can use to identify burnout.

Maslach Burnout Inventory

There's an assessment you can take to determine if you're burned out. The Maslach Burnout Inventory (MBI) was developed by Christina Maslach and her team in 1981.[5] I mention this at the end of this section because this assessment focuses only on work and because it was created so long ago. I believe that burnout for entrepreneurs can come from their personal lives just as often as it can come from their work. However, if you are an individual who likes assessments or needs data to back up what you're already experiencing, the MBI can be very helpful.

Now that you have a path to determine if you are beyond stressed, let's identify your types and timeline of burnout.

DETERMINE THE TYPE OF BURNOUT

There are three types of burnout—attentional, emotional, and physical—and you can experience all three types at once. There are two burnout time frames: acute and chronic. In this section, the goal is for you to identify which types of burnout you may be experiencing. These types usually, but not always, show up in the order presented here.

Identify Attentional Burnout in Yourself

You can find a lot of scientific research to prove that attentional burnout and emotional burnout exist separately from physical burnout, but a story from 2016, published by the Association for Psychological Science, summarizes in detail what we know inherently:

Burnout has a negative impact on brains, especially our attention-capabilities and our emotions. The good news is, it can be reversed.[6]

We're going to look at attentional burnout first because it tends to manifest before the other types. Attentional burnout reduces or eliminates a business owner's ability to focus, communicate clearly, make decisions, and innovate. How I often summarize attentional burnout is that it's the equivalent of an athlete going through a "slump."

One of the clearest outward signs that entrepreneurs are struggling with attentional burnout is that they are not clear and concise in their communication. The ability to share the mission, vision, and values of their business escapes them. They're not firing on all cylinders. This often means their team isn't firing on all cylinders, either, because the business owner doesn't have the capacity to give them the tools they need.

A Surgeon with a Dull Scalpel

Sometimes when a business owner recognizes burnout, it can be a difficult lesson to learn. Trish Saemann, founder of GoBeyond SEO, is a wife, mom, and fantastic leader to her team. She's also a ball of energy wrapped in a firecracker, but even she has experienced burnout. Trish recalls an eye-opening moment when she recognized she was burned out: "I noticed I had made some mistakes in work I had done for a client; I hadn't instructed my team correctly." This is a big part of our job as leaders—providing direction and guardrails for those we lead. Trish compared this burnout to being a surgeon with a dull scalpel. She said, "I needed to step away and make space to figure it out. Not just for me, but for everyone I serve and lead—my clients, my team, my family, and myself."

Another outward sign of attentional burnout is that you've stopped thinking big and aren't innovating within your business. The business may start to feel stuck to everyone working there, including you.

When a business owner has attentional burnout, they will often struggle to make decisions or come up with solutions. They find it hard to concentrate. In my personal experience, I know I have attentional burnout when I'm constantly chasing new ideas instead of working within an existing plan.

When we are dealing with this type of burnout, we tend to be less productive because we experience difficulty with focus. We may be working the same (or more) hours as before, but we're getting less done.

Attentional burnout often means just going through the motions at work. And the biggest risk of attentional burnout is stagnation in your business.

Here are a few questions that you can ask yourself to help you identify if you're going through attentional burnout.

Question	Things to Consider
Are you suffering from the "ins"?	Struggling with inaction, indecision, and indifference are common signs. You find it hard to act. It takes you longer to make decisions, or you feel like you never have enough information to decide. You may also display indifference. For example, you say things like "You figure it out, I don't really have an opinion" when someone asks for feedback.
What is the vision of your business?	If you own and manage an established company and can't answer this question in two sentences, you're probably dealing with attentional burnout.

Question	Things to Consider
When was the last time you had an innovative idea that came to fruition?	Some ideas aren't meant to be, but the important thing here is noting how long it's been since you've had an innovative idea to which you allotted some time for planning and feasibility analysis. If you haven't had a new idea for your business in over six months, you may be experiencing attentional burnout.

Answering these questions can help you identify if you are experiencing this type of burnout, as well as which symptoms you have. Now that we've discussed attentional burnout in detail, let's look at emotional burnout.

Identify Emotional Burnout in Yourself

Emotional burnout is when you feel worn out emotionally. Your body may not be tired, but your capacity to feel emotions is little to none. When people say, "I don't have any more spoons (or f**ks) to give," that is emotional burnout. This type of burnout usually follows attentional burnout, but sometimes it shows up alongside it.

Other signs of emotional burnout include pessimism, detachment, increased irritability, apathy, and a loss of enjoyment—just to name a few.[7]

Out of all the burnout types, this one is the trickiest to identify because it's the easiest to hide from yourself and from others. We have so much on our plates already that our emotions can easily get buried. Therefore, it's important to know the signs of this type of burnout before it explodes. If left unchecked, emotional burnout can lead to a very toxic workplace environment.

Internal Signs of Emotional Burnout

When you are a business owner dealing with emotional burnout, you may feel emotions that you want or need to share but don't. You may rehearse challenging conversations but never actually have those conversations, sweeping those thoughts and feelings under the rug. CEOs dealing with this type of burnout usually have some mechanism of distracting themselves with other activities to escape their feelings.

On the flip side of that, I've had the experience where I go numb and don't have any emotions about anything. This shows up in making poor choices or taking the easy way out. For example, I may not respond to emails from clients for a week or more. I also tend to prioritize comfort over progress in my personal health. I stop caring about the food I put into my body, just as long as I'm not hungry.

Another common internal sign of emotional burnout in entrepreneurs is that they experience consecutive weeks or months when they don't want to go to work. Some days, they wonder why they're even going to work at all.

When a business owner is struggling with emotional burnout, they often feel rudderless and have lost their internal sense of direction.

Friendly, Not Friends

Travis Rosbach says, "Somebody has to be the parent. Somebody has to be the captain. A business owner must be able to say, 'We're not doing blue; we're doing green.' It can be really difficult—early on, I was friends with many of the people I hired. But the day came when I realized I can be friendly with my employees, but I can't be friends with them." Setting this "friendly, not friends" boundary for the first time as a business owner can often lead to emotional burnout because it's a very difficult transition to make. Going from being friends with those who work for you to establishing your boundaries as "the boss" can make you come to hate "the baby"—the business you've built—because you no longer have the same friendly camaraderie at work.

This team-related scenario happens almost inevitably for most founders, and there are a few actions that can help prevent it from developing into burnout. Address the issue early—establish that you're friendly, but not friends. Also, make sure your team members at work are not your only support structure for work-related challenges. As soon as possible, join a mastermind or networking group of other entrepreneurs where you can discuss your business issues. Finally, have clear job descriptions and an evaluation process for everyone who works at your company. That helps remove emotions from any challenging conversations you may need to have regarding performance.

External Signs of Emotional Burnout

While there are many clear internal signs of emotional burnout to look out for in yourself, there can be subtle external symptoms you can track as well.

A scenario that can indicate emotional burnout is when business owners "fall out of love" with their businesses, and it often starts with how you work with the people you lead.

Externally, business owners experiencing emotional burnout are often irritable and anxious or totally checked out and robotic. Sometimes both. Most visionary owners I know don't "sweat the small stuff" and are very engaging in conversation. If their demeanor changes from calm and charming to irritable, anxious, or checked out, that's a red flag.

While the signs of emotional burnout can include being checked out, inactive, and indecisive, it may also show up as micromanagement. This is another external sign of this type of burnout for company owners that others can easily see. You weren't previously prone to micromanaging, but now you're down in the weeds with your team, second-guessing their decisions, watching over their shoulders, or overriding their work altogether. You can't let go of the work. We often don't recognize we are doing it, but our people do.

So how can you tell if you're dealing with emotional burnout? Along with checking for the above signs, I find that asking the following questions can help.

Question	Things to Consider
Is work something you get to do or something you have to do?	For business owners struggling with emotional burnout, it's common for their role to feel like something they have to do. This is hard to admit, but if you feel like you're only going to work to get a paycheck, that's a red flag. Everyone has an off day here and there, so ask this question several times over a two-week period.
Do you care about your business, yourself, and/or others?	Indifference is a common theme with emotional burnout. If the answer to this question is "No," "I don't know if I care," or "I can't afford to care right now," that's a red flag.
What are your first thoughts about work in the morning?	It may not be the first thing you think about in the morning, but when you do think about work, what are you thinking? If it's resentment, longing to do something else, micromanaging others, or just refusing to go to work that day, you may be emotionally burned out.

Now, let's move on to the third type, physical burnout.

Identifying Physical Burnout in Yourself

Physical burnout is the easiest type to recognize. You will feel it, and the people around you will see it. There are a lot of ways it manifests for entrepreneurs, but at its core, physical burnout is when part of a person's body stops working the way it should. It may stop working altogether until the burnout is addressed.

Physical burnout usually shows up last, after attentional and emotional burnout. Our attention span and our feelings will show warning signs, but if we don't pay attention to them, our body will make us pay attention.

"My Right Arm Didn't Work for Two and a Half Years"

When I spoke with Trish Saemann about burnout, she recalled a time when she wasn't exactly sure what was going on with her body, but something was clearly wrong.

"My right arm didn't work for about two and a half years. I was in a sling. I saw several doctors and none of them could identify what was wrong with my arm. I remember telling the doctors, 'I promise you something is wrong,' but I still couldn't find answers."

When part of your body stops working, that might be a sign of burnout!

After a bit more time, Trish realized that the dysfunction in her right arm was due to burnout. She wasn't overusing it in her normal routine and hadn't injured it in an accident. The issue was due to overwhelming, never-ending stress. She laughs now but says, "I'm right-handed and my right hand wasn't working—that was a problem." It was a huge wake-up call for Trish, and she had to figure out how to first recover from burnout and then prevent it altogether.

Trish has several definitions of success these days, but one of them includes mitigating burnout. She wants other business owners to know that "you can run a successful business and not even come close to running yourself ragged." You'll learn more about how Trish achieves this as we go through the book.

The Cleveland Clinic puts fatigue and changes in sleep patterns high on its list of burnout signs.[8] Either you can't get enough sleep or you're sleeping all the time. Personally, I tend to experience both—I can't sleep enough at night, and then I need a nap during the day.

Remember, this is about changes in routines and habits. If you've taken a power nap a few afternoons a week for the last decade, and everything else checks out, that's your routine. But if you rarely nap in the afternoon and start needing one to stay awake later in the day, that's a change to examine.

Another subtle sign that a business owner is dealing with this type of burnout is that they aren't eating well or exercising. All those healthy behaviors we've been told to practice throughout our lifetime take a back seat to work. There are too many physical manifestations of this to mention here, but changes in weight, physical strength, endurance for daily tasks, and the ability to move around are general indicators to explore.

Now that I've shared some of the more subtle signs of physical burnout for business owners, let's discuss the signs that are more noticeable to others.

One of the most obvious signs for otherwise healthy entrepreneurs is that they tend to get sick a lot: colds, the flu, headaches, digestive issues, aches, and pains.[9] In my personal experience, it's like my immune system isn't operating like it should, and I'm more susceptible to short-term illnesses. Colds tend to last longer than they normally would. My right shoulder (affected by an old sports injury) aches and my back hurts. These are all signs for me that I may be physically burned out.

Another sign that can indicate physical burnout is an overall heaviness in body movement. You walk slower and talk slower, and every part of your body feels heavier than it normally does. Those around you pick up on this heaviness and low energy. Usually those more subtle signs, like poor sleep and not eating well, lead to this heaviness in both how your body feels to you and how your body movement is perceived by others.

There are a few questions a business owner can ask themselves to determine if they are physically burned out.

Question	Things to Consider
Are you happy with your health? Is your current health your ideal health for the long term?	I highly recommend you answer this with a yes or no. The following questions will help you expand your answer to this one. If you have a known health condition, you can change this question slightly to "Are you happy with your health, given your existing condition?" For example, I have asthma. I can't cure it, but I can manage it. Adjust this question to acknowledge what you can and cannot control.
How does it feel when you physically move around?	To identify physical burnout, business owners should learn how to check in with their bodies. One of the easiest ways to do this is to pay attention to how you feel when you move. How does it feel to climb a flight of stairs? How does it feel to clean a room in your house? To walk the dog? To sit at an event (a sporting event, a meal at a restaurant, etc.)?

Can you work at this pace for another two months? Another two years?	If you feel like you could work at your current pace for another two years, you're probably a long way from physical burnout. If you can't maintain this work pace for two months, it's time to enact your prevention plan.

If you've never "checked in" with your body, this can initially be an uncomfortable practice. But our bodies tell us a lot, especially when it comes to burnout—if we just listen. I believe this is a crucial skill for business owners to build. It doesn't take a lot of time, and it doesn't mean you have to meditate. It only requires paying attention to how your body feels when you're doing the things you already do. If something feels off—that's an indication that something *is* off.

If you don't pay attention to what your body tells you, your burnout can get so bad that you could end up in the hospital having a panic attack that seems like a heart attack, like I did. And honestly? I was lucky. It certainly could have been a heart attack or stroke.

———

No matter which types of burnout you experience, you can address and recover from them while continuing to work. It's just that how and when you work will need to be adjusted while you implement this system.

Regardless of burnout type, this book can help you address and recover from existing burnout and help you prevent future cases. I cover all of this in upcoming chapters, but for right now, we need to define one other element of burnout—the two burnout timelines.

UNDERSTANDING BURNOUT TIMELINES

There are two timelines of burnout: acute and chronic.

What Is Acute Burnout?

Acute burnout happens when an immediate, urgent situation arises that triggers an avalanche of stress. The business owner usually doesn't see it coming. And while we try to prepare for most scenarios in our business and personal lives, there will always be surprises. This is the primary reason why I believe burnout is inevitable: we don't have control over and can't be prepared for everything.

The stress that comes from these scenarios is so big and fast that it can cause even the most seasoned company owner to burn out.

Scenarios That Lead to Acute Burnout

What does this look like in a business owner's life? Acute burnout often comes from our personal lives. The following are all examples that either I've experienced or I've known other business owners to experience.

For example, imagine you were working out on the weekend and tore your bicep muscle. Or maybe you suddenly needed your gallbladder removed in emergency surgery. Ordinary but unexpected health issues cause acute burnout for entrepreneurs because they are forced to quickly figure out how to keep their companies moving forward when they're unable to work.

I've also known CEOs who have suddenly been diagnosed with cancer and needed to take six months off work to go through the required treatment. The stress of any unexpected health challenge is enough to cause acute burnout. When you add facing your own mortality into the mix, that's an additional layer of anxiety that gives acute burnout an even bigger impact.

Even though our businesses take up a big part of our life, life still happens around us. The passing of a best friend or spouse, becoming a caregiver to an elderly parent, having a baby—these can all cause a business owner to find themselves in acute burnout.

At work, one of the most common scenarios that causes countless business owners to experience acute burnout is when a key staff member unexpectedly resigns. Those key staff members are crucial to keeping your business running, and you can't even begin to think of how to replace them. Over and over again, this catches business owners by surprise, and no matter how much notice they give you, it never seems like enough time. You try to prepare, but there are just some things you can't prepare for, and this one, losing a key employee, is a big one.

I've also seen founders suffer through acute burnout when they acquire a business to expand their company. This kind of acquisition, something that should be celebrated, is one of the most stressful events a growth-focused entrepreneur will face. Merging offices, staff, cultures, and systems comes with immense stress and can easily cause acute burnout.

One situation that caused me acute burnout was a period of unexpected sales growth after letting go of staff members, coupled with knowing I did not want to rehire for those roles. This caused me acute burnout because it forced me back into a role I had previously delegated (client services). I also had to figure out how to serve the new clients with a smaller staff for the foreseeable future. While this process increased both revenue and profit and forced us to become a more efficient and leaner small business, it was still an expected demand. Sales growth is usually celebrated, but sometimes even that can cause acute burnout for us.

Acute burnout can strike at any time. Good times, bad times—it doesn't discriminate.

Is There Anything Good About Acute Burnout?

The bad thing about acute burnout is that it comes on fast, suddenly, and unexpectedly. It is predictable in life that we'll have to deal with stressors we won't see coming. What we cannot predict is when.

I don't recommend waiting for the other shoe to drop as you go through life. But the positive here is that once you accept that you will need space to handle unexpected, acute burnout, you will learn to leave margins in your life. Another positive? Personal growth. Once you're on the other side of an acute burnout, you'll be wiser and more experienced in navigating the nuances of surprise stressors.

The best thing about acute burnout is that it usually has a clear cause. While the actual triggering scenario will itself often be a big surprise, you'll still be able to point to it as the cause of your acute burnout. And when you know the cause of acute burnout right away, you'll know what problems you need to address to help your business overcome the crisis.

One final reason this rate of burnout can be a positive experience is that it usually teaches us lessons about our businesses—what our companies need—even if the cause of acute burnout is personal. It helps the business owner see their company's (or their own) weaknesses and, if addressed properly, will put them in a better position going forward. Acute burnout teaches business owners what's needed to keep the business running without them.

Acute burnout happens. It's important to embrace that and know how to work with it. If it goes unaddressed, that acute stressor becomes normal. As those stressors start to stack up, a company owner can spiral into chronic burnout—which is usually much more difficult to address.

What Is Chronic Burnout?

Chronic burnout means there's no end in sight. It's not uncommon for business owners to view how they feel during chronic burnout as "normal" for them because they cannot put brackets around when it started and when it will end. Owners experiencing chronic burnout slog through their day-to-day, often thinking, "This is my job. This is what entrepreneurs do."

While chronic burnout could go on and on indefinitely, it usually doesn't. Eventually, something gives. Business owners often become aware of their chronic burnout when their bodies, their minds, or their loved ones say, "Enough is enough." Something big happens—a major medical issue arises, an important personal relationship reaches the verge of collapse, or the business becomes unsustainable for various reasons.

I often think of the difference between acute burnout and chronic burnout in terms of fireworks and dynamite. Acute burnout is like fireworks. It's fast and has a short fuse that ignites quickly. Once it explodes, you know exactly what happened, and then the show is over. Yes, there's an explosion, but it's confined in many ways (time, space, cause, and effect).

Chronic burnout, however, has a long fuse with a pile of dynamite at the end, usually buried under a mountain. It's dangerous because you often can't see whether the fuse has been lit, the length of the fuse, or how much dynamite is at the end of the fuse. You're farther away from the pile of dynamite, so you can't see the explosion coming until it happens. When the dynamite ignites, the explosion is big, has a long-lasting impact, and can be potentially devastating.

With acute burnout the blowup tends to happen right away; in chronic burnout you have a slow burn, and that leads to a shattering explosion.

Scenarios That Lead to Chronic Burnout

Chronic burnout often comes from, surprisingly, the "it is what it is" parts of your business—the way your business has already been operating. I see chronic burnout in business owners who aren't delegating responsibilities. They may not want to hire, or they may not be able to source talent. For some reason, they simply can't or won't let go of certain tasks.

Often, self-made CEOs hit this delegation wall because of money constraints. One thing I always advise founders to do to avoid chronic burnout is to price their products and services to allow for hiring. Even when you're doing all the work and don't have plans to hire, this is still a good practice.

Remember: always give yourself margins.

These are just a few business examples, but there are also personal experiences, both good and challenging, that can cause chronic burnout. For example: becoming a caregiver for an elderly parent (challenging); welcoming a new member to your family (good); outgrowing relationships and forging new ones (both good and challenging); closing on an initial round of seed funding for your company (good); your spouse resigning from their job (challenging and possibly good in the long run); publishing and promoting a book (good).

Chronic burnout can even be caused by too many good things happening all at once!

One of the key takeaways here is that the experiences that cause the chronic timeline don't happen overnight, so addressing and recovering from chronic burnout won't happen overnight, either. I personally experienced chronic burnout after it had been building for four years, and I ended up taking a year to completely recover from it. I've known other business owners for whom it built up for over a decade, and they needed two to three years to address it and fully recover.

The real challenge with chronic burnout is identifying the root causes because, unlike with acute burnout, there isn't usually a singular event that ignites the dynamite. It's a slow burn of a long fuse. Your goal is to identify the cause and address it before it explodes. There's usually more than one cause, and it'll take a good bit of reflection to figure out the causes. In chapter six, I'll offer more insights to help you identify the causes.

Is There Anything Good About Chronic Burnout?

The bad thing about chronic burnout is that it can lead to major crises in one's health, finances, and everything in between. After what I've just described, saying there's anything good that can come from chronic burnout may seem foolish.

There are a few gifts chronic burnout gives us as business owners, however. One, I've found that chronic burnout forces you to prioritize, and it forces you to cut. The end result of this is not work–life balance but work–life harmony. Work–life balance requires calibration and juggling with even the slightest addition to either. Work–life harmony happens when work and life coexist together and there's a peaceful flow of give-and-take.

Another positive is that chronic burnout often helps a business owner become a better leader. I think this happens because a chronic burnout cycle requires us to have compassion for ourselves; we therefore become more compassionate people on the other side of it. It also helps us become better leaders because it often teaches us more about ourselves—who we are, our core values, what brings us joy, what we want our lives to look like, and how we need our businesses to serve us (not the other way around). Knowing ourselves better gives us a greater capacity to lead other people.

Even in the darkest days of chronic burnout, a business owner can find some peace in knowing the lessons they'll learn will be worth it.

CHAPTER TAKEAWAYS

For a business owner to address, overcome, and personally recover from burnout, they must first identify that they are burned out. Sometimes it's hard for business owners to identify this in themselves.

- There are five ways to tell if you're in business owner burnout: the "I miss you" rule, a bad case of the "ins," the "two weeks" rule, the "I'm busy" rule, and the Maslach Burnout Inventory.
- There are three types of burnout: attentional, emotional, and physical. A business owner who is

burned out may experience one, two, or all three of these types of burnout at one time.

- There are two time frames of burnout: acute and chronic. With acute burnout, an event happens that causes an extreme amount of stress and puts the business owner into burnout. In chronic burnout, stress builds up over time.

- Often, there isn't a singular event that causes chronic burnout. Instead, the normal "it is what it is" grind gradually causes it.

CHAPTER 6

Determine Causes and Isolate Your Burnout

Burnout can be caused by a lot of things, as discussed in the previous chapter, which gave you the groundwork to identify if you are a burned-out business owner. Chapter five also helped you define the types and timelines of burnout you may be facing through examples from my experiences and those of other business owners.

Now that you have those definitions, the next steps are to determine the causes of your burnout and isolate your burnout. I've said a few times throughout this book that being burned out doesn't have to mean that you shut down and step away from your business entirely. The secret to pulling this off lies in this chapter.

In this chapter, I'm going to share some thoughts on the difference between stress and burnout. You'll then identify the causes of your burnout. Lastly, I'll teach you a way to isolate your burnout from the rest of your life so that you can continue to work while also addressing the challenges presented during this time.

Chapter Overview

Section	Summary
Identify the Cause of Acute Burnout	How to identify acute burnout, common examples, and one important mistake to avoid.
Identify the Cause of Chronic Burnout	General themes for chronic burnout and how you can pinpoint the cause of it.
Isolate Your Burnout	How to isolate burnout so you can continue working while going through this process (if needed).

Stress Does Not Equal Burnout

It's a safe assumption that we all experience stress. You may feel stressed about a deadline, but once the deadline passes, so does the stress. You may feel anxious about an upcoming doctor appointment, but afterwards you may feel relieved because you have a plan for treatment. Those are just two examples of how stress comes and goes.

Having stress doesn't mean we're burned out. Here's the difference to be aware of: whereas "normal" stress ebbs and flows, never-ending worry that is left unaddressed leads to burnout.

IDENTIFY THE CAUSE
OF ACUTE BURNOUT

Now, let's get into identifying the causes of your burnout. I shared many specific examples in chapter five; here, we'll explore broader categories of possible causes. There are many reasons a business owner might suffer from this immediate and overwhelming disengagement; your causes of acute burnout will be unique to you.

The Causes of Acute Burnout Are (Usually) Obvious

This is how acute burnout typically shows up: You have a manageable level of stress, and you can see an end to each stressor. You have space in your daily life to manage those stressors, to complete work and personal life duties, and to practice some self-care. Then, something big happens in your life—something with an immediate impact on you. Suddenly, you're experiencing signs of burnout. If this describes your current state, you should know the cause—the big event that just happened.

Don't Mistake a Tipping Point for Acute Burnout

It's easy to mislabel an event as the cause of acute burnout when it was actually a tipping point into chronic burnout. For example, let's say you've had chronic stress for a while—a steady undercurrent of medium to high levels of stress—with no end in sight.

Then, suddenly, a key employee leaves, or a loved one passes away, and you go into burnout. This kind of event is more likely to be a tipping point into chronic burnout, not the cause of acute burnout. Yes, there was a clear-cut event that caused you to experience burnout, but there was an underlying state of unending stress before the event took place.

The way you tell the difference is by looking at your stress levels before the precipitating event happened. If you had a low or very manageable level of "normal" stress, you are likely dealing with acute burnout. If you were already struggling, burning the candle at both ends, and regularly displaying red flags and staying in your danger zone (see chapter two), that event was most likely a tipping point into chronic burnout. An event that causes acute burnout is not the same as a sudden situation that pushes long-term stress over the edge into chronic burnout.

What we've gone over in this book thus far has probably given you some ideas for where to look to identify the cause of your acute burnout. If you're struggling with chronic burnout, though, it can be tougher to figure out the cause. You're likely looking for several causes, so let's dig deeper into how to find them.

IDENTIFY THE CAUSE OF CHRONIC BURNOUT

There are many reasons a business owner suffers from the long-lasting and never-ending state of chronic burnout. It is the result of stress that has built up over time and has not been addressed with a plan to resolve or manage it. In addition to some of the examples already given in chapter five, here are a few broader categories that can cause chronic burnout:

Common Categories	Explanation
Lack of progress in business, despite your best efforts	Sometimes you know why your business is not progressing, and you can live with it. But if, despite your and your team's best efforts, the business does not progress, disengagement may follow.
Lack of fulfillment at work	If you aren't fulfilled by the work you do in your business, that's a problem. This can go on for a while before you realize it, and then identifying how to correct it can take a lot of effort. That's a perfect recipe for chronic burnout.

Unrealistic expectations	These may be unrealistic expectations someone else has of you, but with entrepreneurs, I've seen it more frequently as unrealistic expectations of themselves.
Values misalignment	If your work does not align with your personal values, or if your personal life and relationships do not align with your values, over time this can lead to burnout.

When you're in the time frame of chronic burnout, there hasn't been an ebb and flow of stress. You've been in a steady (or increasing) state of overwhelm. It's become your status quo.

Sometimes the industry alone can cause burnout. As Trish Saemann from GoBeyond SEO puts it, "In the marketing industry, every day there's something new. We often don't have the capacity to keep up—we don't have any fuel left to burn. But it's our job to keep up with our education, and in a constantly changing industry like digital marketing, that alone can cause burnout."

Chronic burnout seeps into all areas of your life—both work and personal—so it can be difficult to untangle. You might wonder, "Was it an ongoing business stressor that caused my chronic burnout, which then caused my personal-life stress, which added fuel to the fire? Or was it long-standing personal stress that built up and caused me to burn out, which showed up in that business problem? Or have I experienced stress for so long due to [fill in the blank] that it finally caused chronic burnout?"

In my experience, there's usually a stacking of several stressors. At this point, if you're unsure about whether you're dealing with acute or chronic burnout, the following steps will make that clear for you.

And if you're facing chronic burnout, the following process will help you identify the cause of it.

Let's get to the bottom of this, shall we?

Temporarily Get Away from Stress Zones to a Place Where You Feel Calm

Get away from your workplace and from places that could be a source of personal stress—your stress zones. Go to a place where you feel calmer and take something to write notes in or on. There's also a section for this in the free workbook guide (see the introduction for instructions on how to get yours).

For me, this place is my backyard or out on a lake on my paddle-board. For another business owner, it's her pontoon boat. Another goes to a park. Another goes to their sister's house. Wherever you feel calmer and can forget about work and personal stress for a bit—that's the place where you want to go.

This does not require a vacation or even a day off. If you've made enough space in chapter four to give yourself a day off, now would be a good time to use it, but that's not required.

Wherever you go, it needs to be away from your stress in a place where you feel calmer.

Identify What or Who Stressed You Out and What You Think About It

Now that you're in a place where you feel less stressed, what or who is missing from that place? What have you temporarily escaped?

The answer to this question is often a good indicator as to the direction of the stress that caused chronic burnout. While you may not be able to identify the exact stressor at this stage, your answer here will provide a place to start. For example, you may have tempo-rarily escaped work. You do not know specifically what you escaped at work, but you know that the stress is much worse while you're at work. Therefore, the stressor at this point is work.

Once you identify a stressor, note three thoughts or feelings you have when you think about dealing with it. No judgment here—you are the only person who will see this list. We are going to work through an additional step with each of the thoughts or feelings you note here, so that's why I limit it to three. You can repeat these steps for your other top stressors after you work through the process one time.

Ask "Why?" Three Times

Now that you have your list of three thoughts or feelings about that one stressor, you're going to ask, "Why?" for each of those thoughts or feelings. And you're going to ask this three times.

When you ask, "Why?" repeatedly, you'll get beyond the surface level of the thought or feeling, and that will help you identify the cause of your chronic burnout. Each answer to "Why?" will form the next "Why?" question. You go a little deeper each time you ask the question—it's like peeling back the layers of an onion.

For example, let's say one of my feelings from the previous step is "frustrated" with the lack of growth at my company. Here's an exam-ple of this step with that feeling:

Why #1: Why am I frustrated? Because I have zero enjoyment in my business.
Why #2: Why do I have zero enjoyment at work? I feel like I'm always putting out fires and never get to the important work.

Why #3: Why am I always putting out fires and not getting to
the important work? Because someone has to do it (aha!),
and, if I'm honest, I don't manage my time well (aha!). I
prioritize fighting fires over tackling important work.

As you answer these "Why?" questions, you'll most likely see common themes. Whereas acute burnout is caused by a specific event,
chronic burnout usually comes from recurring patterns and routines.

At this point, you probably have a good idea as to what's causing your chronic burnout. If you're still struggling, though, consider
these three common sources of chronic burnout for business owners:
people at work, processes, and personal factors.

- **People at work** include all the people who work for or with
  you. This can include employees, subcontractors, key vendors,
  clients, business partners, investors, shareholders, and so on.
- **Processes** cause burnout when steps in a business process
  aren't working or when there's no process to follow. If
  you're the founder, this usually lands on your plate, but you
  often don't have the time or resources to deal with process
  problems, so they go unresolved until something breaks.
  Once something breaks, you don't have the capacity to keep
  up with work. Alternatively, you might have a process that's
  so outdated or nonexistent that it causes a plethora of other
  problems in your business.
- Finally, a **personal** challenge or issue can cause burnout. You
  may be going through a divorce, having a baby, or becoming
  a caregiver for an aging parent. Other examples that can
  disrupt your business and cause burnout include moving,

deployments, deaths, and medical crises. These elements may start in your personal life, but they can easily cascade into your business.

Once you think through this, document a few themes that are coming up for you as causes of chronic burnout, as well as any specific events that may have contributed to burnout. I've found that if a business owner is honest with themselves and trusts their gut, they should know at this point what's causing their chronic burnout.

Example in Action

Here's what the three steps to identify causes of chronic burnout look like in practice. This is a personal example that I went through after my trip to the emergency room.

After taking a day off work, I went to my "away from stress" and "calmer" place, and I wrote down how I was feeling: frustrated, tired, and unsure.

Then I asked, "Why?" three times for each of those feelings. Here's what that looked like.

Feeling	Asking "Why?" Three Times
Frustrated	Why? I just can't seem to get ahead, no matter what I do. Why? The things I do make sense on paper, but when we implement, they don't work. Why? Something might be getting lost in translation between the plan and the implementation (process).
Tired	Why? I'm not sleeping well. Why? I have poor sleep habits. Why? I don't turn off my brain early enough in the evening, and I stay "plugged in" to my phone. I also work late because I feel I'm constantly behind. I wake up on my own after only five hours of sleep.

Feeling	Asking "Why?" Three Times
Unsure	Why? Nothing has worked. Why? Maybe I'm not the one who can grow the company. Why? Maybe I lack the experience needed to elevate the company into the next growth stage.

Do you see a common theme here? I do. I was trying to solve all the problems myself without asking for help, even though I needed it. I also felt like I had asked for this job as a business owner and a specific set of responsibilities that came with it. To top it all off, I had zero boundaries when it came to sleep.

If I had to narrow down the causes for my burnout here, it would be a lack of boundaries and not asking for help.

Go through this exercise for yourself, and once you get to the end of it, you'll see at least one common theme emerge that will help you identify what caused your chronic burnout.

Once you've identified your causes, you'll be ready to isolate your burnout.

ISOLATE YOUR BURNOUT

Now that you can more clearly see what caused your burnout, we're going to isolate it. Why do we do this? To keep your burnout from burning you or your business to the ground. This is a crucial step that will enable you to compartmentalize it.

Most of us agree that our thoughts and words mean something to us—they affect us in some way. Our words also affect the people around us who hear them. Because thoughts and words have real impacts, we're going to use them to help ourselves (and others) isolate our burnout work from everything else going on in our lives. This will help you put it away when you need to and work on it within the space you've made to do so.

This is how you regain some control while also dealing with burnout.

Isolate Your Burnout Words

Isolating your words is trickier than it sounds. Sometimes you will have planned time to talk about your burnout (perhaps with your leadership team, in therapy, or with your BFF). Other times, you may find those specific words spontaneously come up in conversations. It's important to isolate your burnout words from the rest of your words, no matter when and how they come up.

I've also found that doing this over time helps reduce any guilt or embarrassment you might feel about your burnout.

How Do You Isolate Your Burnout Words?

First, become aware of the words you use when you talk about your burnout. Depending on who you're talking with, you may not use the word *burnout* itself—instead, you may find yourself using words like *overwhelmed, stressed, frustrated, fatigued, concerned, exhausted, disengaged*, and *worried*. If you identify the words you use to indicate burnout, you'll begin to notice when you're talking about it. The other people in the conversation don't have to know you're using burnout words; what's important is that you know. Then, when you're having conversations and find yourself using those words, go ahead and call it what it is. Recognize it. It can even be something as short as,

"Wow, I've said the word *stressed* several times already—I'm dealing with some burnout."

Or, if you enter a conversation and you want to talk about your burnout, say that up front. That might sound like, "I'd like to discuss my burnout as part of our meeting today so that we can plan accordingly." If you aren't comfortable using the term *burnout*, find another term that you are comfortable using. The words *stress*, *overwhelmed*, *fatigue*, *concern*, *exhausted*, *disengaged*, and *worry* are some possible substitutes.

Finally, get back to your non-burnout work. After you've acknowledged that you're using burnout words (whether out loud or to yourself), give those burnout words a little time to settle. For example, imagine you are talking with a trusted member of your leadership team and you say something like, "I'm overwhelmed with the changes we're making in the company." You recognize that you used the word *overwhelmed*. Once the conversation ends, on your way back to your office, you note to yourself that you said a burnout word and that you expressed your burnout to someone else. Let that sink in. Depending on the conversation, it might take as little as ten seconds to notice this. After it sinks in that you mentioned your burnout, you put that thought away and return to your non-burnout work. Remember, you've made space to work on burnout, so you'll revisit that work when it's time.

"And Then" Isolation

Frank Schwartz did an excellent job at isolating burnout words and thoughts, even though he didn't know it at the time. He had a realization about two simple words used together: "and then." Frank shared this example to illustrate:

"I'll prove to my dad and to everyone around me that I'm successful because I've accumulated all these things, AND THEN I'll have their approval." It may also sound like, "I will achieve or accumulate XYZ, AND THEN I'll be happy, or AND THEN they'll love me."

Frank's illustration of how these two words were so closely tied to why he was burned out is a perfect example of isolating your burnout words and thoughts from everything else. From there, it became about getting beyond the "and thens" so that Frank could finally see that he was enough just as he was.

Now that we've walked through isolating burnout words, we'll go through a similar exercise to isolate your burnout thoughts.

How Do You Isolate Your Burnout Thoughts?

Admittedly, this can be challenging to do at first. If you're anything like me, your mind can go from thought to thought very quickly without a break in between. I can also get very focused on fixing a problem (like what is causing my burnout) and lose focus on everything else.

"Who Am I to Judge?"

Trish Saemann has some very specific thoughts that indicate she's burned out. I think many business owners experience these burnout thoughts but aren't willing to admit it. Trish says, "I know I'm burned out when I become resentful toward others' joy in their downtime. I find myself thinking that those individuals don't work hard enough to get to enjoy themselves that much. They don't deserve that vacation. That's when I have to take a step back and ask myself, 'Who am I to judge?' That is the insidious part of burnout for me—I start resenting other people who are not burned out."

It's helpful when we can label our thoughts and decide if we want to address those thoughts at a given time. Burnout thoughts will pop up during times when you're not working on addressing your burnout. Decide ahead of time what you want to do with those thoughts. Once I recognize a burnout thought, I imagine it on a theater screen passing by like a scene in a movie.

Some people may want to jot down their burnout thoughts as they come up and then return to their other work. If you think there's a chance you'll chase that burnout thought down a rabbit hole, or if you feel worried about forgetting it, note that thought and save it for later.

Now that you know what you'll do with burnout thoughts when they arise, it's time to practice recognizing and categorizing your thoughts. For example, if you have a thought about upcoming travel, label it as a "travel thought." A thought about your spouse? Maybe that's defined as a "relationship thought." *Do not* characterize these thoughts as good or bad. You are simply recognizing and categorizing thoughts as they pop up.

Once your thoughts are labeled and compartmentalized, you can get back to what you were doing before those interruptive burnout thoughts showed up. That's how you isolate burnout thoughts and put them away until it's their turn to get your attention.

"What's the Worst That Can Happen?"

When I spoke with Scott McIntosh, the founder of DigitalTreehouse and inventor of Cell Phone Seat, he admitted, "I'm in burnout right now. I've got seven text messages, thirty-seven emails, and nine phone calls, and I need to address all of them. I need to review a thirty-eight-page contract. These are all important for my businesses, but I'm overwhelmed and I find *it really hard to do any of them." Many business owners can relate to this story.*

What's helped Scott continue to work while he's experiencing burnout are a few things. First, he says, "When I'm approaching the end of the day, I ask myself, 'If I don't complete tasks that are left on my list, what is the worst that can happen?' It's usually nothing—nothing will happen. That has helped me step away and also really see that some work can wait."

He also tries to focus on what he did accomplish when he looks back at his day or week instead of focusing on what he did not. He says, "If you look back at your week and see what you did get accomplished, that's important. Instead of getting to Friday and focusing on those two emails you didn't answer, and then being stressed all weekend because of those two emails, focus on what you got done, not those two emails. That helps me feel a lot better."

Why Is Isolating Burnout Helpful?

Isolating your burnout is what enables you to keep working while you are addressing and recovering from it.

Isolating burnout words from the words you use for other topics helps delineate burnout from the rest of your life. It helps you be more in control of your conversations. It also helps you own your burnout and reminds you that you're doing something about it.

You might be a burned-out business owner, but you are still a business owner.

Even in that sentence, do you feel the difference? Separating "business owner" from "burned-out"—powerful, right? Yes, you are both of those things together, *and* you are both of those things separately. Isolating your burnout helps you continue to be the entrepreneur you are.

Isolating your burnout thoughts from your other thoughts gives your brain a break from thinking about burnout. It also helps you remember that you have made space for your burnout while also continuing to have space for some work and personal-life duties.

This practice helps you focus during a time when it may be really hard to do so. It helps untangle burnout from everything else in your life. It can help remove the emotional charge from burnout. You're dealing with words and thoughts—that's it. They are neither good nor bad. You'll address them in the space you've set aside. Work on them within that space and then put them down for a while. That way, you won't ruminate about your burnout.

Isolating your burnout words and thoughts may initially be an uncomfortable exercise, but the rewards are worth it. By isolating both, you're doing two very important things.

One, you are actively practicing being aware of your burnout even when no one else is looking. That is integrity.

Two, by isolating your burnout through these exercises, you're keeping it from taking over your life. This is how you continue to live and work while also addressing and overcoming your burnout.

CHAPTER TAKEAWAYS

Identifying the cause of your burnout is an important step in the burnout-battling process. There are many common causes. It's important to remember that stress does not equal burnout and to learn how to distinguish between the two.

- The cause of chronic burnout is usually harder to identify than the cause of acute burnout. Chronic burnout for most business owners usually originates in one of three areas—people at work, processes, or personal factors.

- Isolating your burnout is how you can continue to work and participate in your personal life while also addressing your burnout. In this regard, compartmentalizing burnout from everything else in your life is an invaluable skill for busy entrepreneurs.

- To isolate burnout, first learn how to isolate your burnout words from other words you use in conversation. Then, learn how to isolate your burnout thoughts from other thoughts. By practicing these two techniques, business owners can prevent their burnout from taking over every part of their lives.

CHAPTER 7

Address the Problems
Burnout Creates

Addressing the problems involved in your burnout is about
fixing those problems, not about your personal recovery (we will get
to that in chapter eight). These two actions are often lumped together
in other resources, but they are two different steps in this book.

I've found that business owners have a hard time focusing on their
personal recovery if they do not at least begin to address the problems
surrounding their burnout (especially if their companies are experiencing problems), so that's why we start here. After we address the
problems, you can move forward into recovering from burnout.

Is this chapter about your business or about you? Good question.
The problems may be in your business, in your personal life, or perhaps both. As entrepreneurs, we generally find that our work and
personal lives are intertwined. A problem in one will most certainly
affect the other.

It's also important to know that sometimes the problems and challenges you'll address in this chapter can precede a burnout. It's also true that a burnout can cause the problems. It doesn't matter which came first. What matters is that you address the problems, whether they came before or after the burnout.

In this chapter, you'll address any problem or crisis that has come up in this course of burnout. If you're dealing with acute burnout, there's a clear crisis that put you into burnout. If you have chronic burnout, there are probably multiple crises that caused stress to turn into burnout. We'll tackle these crises in two parts. First, there's the quick-fix plan. Then, there's the longer-term solution to the challenges you're facing.

Chapter Overview

Section	Summary
Step 1: Assemble Your Solutions Team	Why you assemble your team first and who should be on this team.
Step 2: Identify the Urgent Problem	How to identify a problem with your team's help.
Step 3: Create a Quick-Fix Crisis Plan Step 4: Implement Your Quick-Fix Plan, Observe, and Review	Why you use a quick fix initially, how to create and start the plan, and what to observe during implementation.
Step 5: Ask Your Team to Create a Long-Term Plan	How to step back and provide the framework to your team so that they can create a long-term plan for the problem.

One Chapter, Two Plans

We'll first create a quick-fix, temporary plan. Band-Aids exist to stop the bleeding. They are not meant to be permanent; neither is the temporary plan.

To address the urgent problems surrounding your burnout, a temporary plan is okay at first. In my experience, it's preferred for two reasons. First, it usually takes fewer resources from you (and everyone else) to create. Even if you know you'll have to undo it later to implement a permanent fix, stopping a problem's momentum is your first goal. Use what you already have to do so.

The other reason a temporary plan is preferable at this point is speed. It stops the situation more quickly than a plan that takes longer to create and implement would. That longer-term plan will be needed—just not initially. This temporary fix will give you the space you and your team need to create a longer-term plan and get you recovering from burnout more quickly.

For example, if the major software system that runs your operations suddenly crashes, that's a crisis that could cause acute burnout. The temporary plan is to get your operations running again. Yes, a long-term plan to figure out what happened and prevent it in the future is needed. But to stop the problem in its tracks, you need to get operations up and running again, so that's what you do first.

Now, let's dive into the steps to address the problems caused by your burnout.

STEP 1: ASSEMBLE YOUR SOLUTIONS TEAM

The first step in creating your response plan is to assemble the response team. Ask for help from those around you whom you trust. You may have already assembled this team in prior chapters. If you've done the work outlined thus far, your team will likely involve the same people you've been leaning on.

If you're dealing with a business crisis, your team will be people in or around your business—key employees and staff, business partners, and strategic advisors. If you're dealing with a personal crisis, your team will include people from your personal support system—your spouse / significant other, best friend, therapist/counselor, and family members. If you're dealing with problems both at work and at home, you'll have two teams.

The Importance of Your Team

When I asked Frank Schwartz what got him out of burnout, he listed a few things—coaching, self-reflection, and changing his definition of success. But the one he elaborated the most on was the support of the team he retained at LEC Media.

He recalls, "I would go into the office and tell them, 'Guys, it is over. This is ending. You should go and get jobs.' But my staff had an unfaltering belief in me, so they stayed. They would say, 'You'll be back. We think you'll be back.'"

Frank says that it meant so much to have people at work, people you lead, who believe in you even when you don't believe in yourself. "It was nice to have people who were in it with me, at work, who saw all the bad but stuck around because they believed in me. That is what really pulled me out of this burnout."

It's okay to tell these people that you're dealing with a problem and need help, no matter the origin. You need help here; ask for it.

Can You Get Vulnerable with This Team?

Building a leadership team you can be vulnerable with is crucial for Meghan Lynch. She describes this team as "people I do not need to posture in front of, or who are looking to me to have all the answers. These are people who can hear me struggle with something and come toward me with support and ownership and be in it with me."

You assemble your team first because they can take a much more objective look at the problem. They may see something you haven't noticed yet and can get closer to the source of the issue without experiencing as much stress as you might.

An Example to Illustrate Why You Assemble Your Team First

Imagine you're cooking at home. Suddenly, there's a small grease fire on your cooktop. Even though you know the fire is the real problem, your initial reactions will be to the heat and the smoke alarm. It may take you a few seconds to grab the fire extinguisher or throw baking soda on that fire.

If someone else is in the kitchen with you—someone who isn't as close to the flames—they can act more quickly than you can to address the fire (the real problem). They'll have a different, more objective perspective on the issue at hand than you will because they aren't as close to it. They may be the one who gets the fire extinguisher. Or they may say something to get your attention back on the fire instead of on the smoke alarm.

If you try to identify the problems you're facing before assembling your team, you may end up focusing on the smoke alarm or staying away from the flames. A team assembled in advance can help draw your attention back to the actual crisis—the fire.

Now that you have your team assembled, you can work together to identify the crisis.

STEP 2: IDENTIFY THE URGENT PROBLEM

To identify an urgent problem, your team will first review the current situation.

At work, let's say a key employee has resigned. The crisis you may have identified at this point is that someone with an immense amount of knowledge and expertise is leaving your company. That will require a longer-term solution. However, the urgent problem your solutions team will identify is that there needs to be a short-term plan to get the former employee's work done.

For a personal-life example, imagine that you have kids. One day, the wheels fall off—literally. You get a flat tire while on your way to pick up your kids from school. You identify the crisis as not picking up your kids on time.

You pull over to the side of the road, call a member of your support network, and begin to tell them what happened. You say, "I have a flat tire, I'm on the side of the road, and I can't get to the kids."

What's the first thing they'll say? It won't be, "Oh no! The kids will be waiting!" The first thing they'll say will be, "Oh no! Are you okay?"

The real crisis isn't getting to the kids on time; it's your safety. You won't see it until your support team sees it. Then you'll work out a plan for your safety, and then the kids.

There aren't many "steps" to identifying the real, urgent problem at hand. You give your team the overview of what's going on from your perspective. Your team will look around and see things you don't. They'll bring that information back to the entire solutions team, including you.

Then you'll identify the real crisis, which becomes the focal point through the rest of this section.

STEP 3: CREATE A QUICK-FIX CRISIS PLAN

Now that you and your team know the real crisis, you can create a temporary plan. You have the who (team) and the why (crisis). Now you need what, when, where, and how.

Identify the following:

- The actions needed to stop this issue from spiraling further (note: this temporary plan isn't meant to completely fix the problem)
- The order of those actions and when they will be completed
- The resources needed to take those actions
- Who is responsible for each action, including acquiring the necessary resources

Culture-Gap Analysis Was a Quick Fix

For Meghan Lynch, there was specific work she did to address the toxic culture at her workplace, which was a big step in addressing her burnout. She explains:

"There was just this tipping point where I created this big spreadsheet of all the current things that were happening in the business that were not what I wanted. I made a list of the negatives with no judgment. And then I made a list of all the things that I wanted my business to be.

"I got really, really clear on where we were and where we needed to be. I did a culture-gap analysis on my own business. And then I created an action plan for each item that would move us from where we were to where we wanted to be."

That initial gap analysis was part of Meghan's quick-fix plan. From there, Meghan says that she spent a year leading herself and her team through those action items and that by the end of that year she once again was excited to go to work. She and her team had changed Six-Point Creative's culture from a toxic one to one where people, including Meghan, looked forward to working each day.

The temporary plan you create will vary greatly for each problem, but any plan you make should have just one purpose: to stop the problem from continuing. Once you have your plan documented, you're ready for the next step.

STEP 4: IMPLEMENT YOUR QUICK-FIX PLAN, OBSERVE, AND REVIEW

Set the temporary plan in motion and follow it. There may be times when you'll need to adjust, which is fine. These plans are short for several reasons. One of those reasons is that there are usually some unknowns when you get started with implementation, so remaining flexible is important.

Observe

During this implementation, part of your role as a leader is to observe. Pay specific attention to:

- Unexpected other challenges that come up
- Additional resources needed that weren't initially planned
- Any confusion that arises for your team
- Any steps that were added to, changed from, or removed from the initial temporary plan

These observations will help your team create a long-term plan to fully address the cause of the problem and prevent it from happening again. Right now, observe and take notes when you see any of these elements come up during the implementation of the quick-fix plan. Hang on to that list; we'll need it in the next step.

Review Observations

Your team implemented the short-term solution. You feel a noticeable de-escalation in stress right now with just the temporary plan in place. Now it's time to review what you observed throughout the implementation.

First, you'll have a debrief meeting with your team. Get together with them and discuss your observations. Those items I asked you to observe above are great conversation starters here. Reviewing your implementation will help your team build the long-term plan in step five.

Highlight Anything You'd Change Now

During the debrief meeting, also work with your team to identify anything you would change in the initial quick-fix plan. Now that you've gone through the plan, in hindsight you and your team will likely find a couple of things you would have done differently. That's valuable knowledge to gather from your team (and yourself).

This is how a process gets better—reviewing it with experience on your side. Armed with this intel, you're ready to create a longer-term solution to the underlying causes of the problem.

The Tipping Point, Round Two

As you and your team stop the urgent problem, you'll eventually have a moment when you feel like you've gotten to the other side of the problem.

When you reach that moment, take a breath. Do something that helps you recognize and celebrate that the immediate crisis is almost over. You could take the solutions team out to lunch or give them a bonus or an extra day off. You could also celebrate this moment by treating yourself to a night out with your friends, a massage, or a new book. Take a beat to celebrate this positive tipping point.

At the end of this step, your urgent issues will have been addressed. The issue at hand may not be entirely fixed yet, but you have a team working on it. Eventually, however, the real, underlying problem that caused the crisis will need to be addressed.

STEP 5: ASK YOUR TEAM TO CREATE A LONG-TERM PLAN

At this point, your involvement with addressing the problem will be dramatically reduced. You need to recover from the burnout—to take care of yourself personally. You and your team have addressed the immediate pain and stress of the crisis, and you've debriefed the initial quick-fix plan results and learned some important lessons.

Now it's time to let this project go for a while. Except for checking in at agreed-upon times, this is your team's work. The actions they'll take include:

1. Determining how long the quick fix is sustainable
2. Walking back several steps from the problem
3. Naming the *real* problem
4. Creating and implementing a long-term plan

Let's take a closer look at each; this is a guide you can give to your solutions team to help them do this work.

Determine How Long the Quick Fix Is Sustainable

Determining how long the temporary fix can hold is first on this list for a couple of reasons.

One, the quick fix may be the final fix. Or maybe it only needs a few minor adjustments to become the long-term solution.

Two, this step helps determine how quickly the team will need to move through finding and implementing a longer-term solution. This will tell your team how much time they (and you) have between now and when the quick-fix solution will stop working. That amount of time is a crucial variable to know at this point.

Walk Back Several Steps from the Problem

Now that your team knows how much time they have, they'll work on identifying the source of the crisis. They'll do this by backtracking from the crisis to get to the cause.

I suggest asking, "Why?" three times to backtrack to the underlying cause. Below are a couple of examples.

Work Crisis: Key Employee Resigns

A key employee resigns, causing a crisis for your business and burnout for you.

Why did the key employee resign? He felt limited in some way at work (salary, growth opportunities, benefits, flexible work arrangement, etc.) and secured a role at another organization.

Why did he feel limited at your business? Because he *was* limited. Your organization didn't have a structure in place to support his growth.

Why doesn't your organization have a support structure for the growth of key employees like him? It doesn't have the resources to support it.

Personal Crisis: Flat Tire / Kids Stuck at School

You were driving to pick up your kids from school and your tire blew out. This created a crisis and threw you into burnout.

Why did the flat tire happen? There may not be a real reason—it just happened. It's a normal experience, though it created a crisis.

Why did a normal experience create a crisis? Because your kids were stuck at school for a while, you had to juggle their after-school care, and you needed to get your car out of the ditch. That threw off the rest of your afternoon and evening, as well as the next day.

Why did the disruption of your schedule throw off the rest of that day and part of the next day, too? Because you had so many things to do in a specific order—so much so that one disruption, like getting a flat tire, messed up your entire week.

Now that we've walked through the "Why?" exercise for a few examples, let's move on to the next item for planning a longer-term solution.

Name the *Real* Problem

The real problem may have already jumped out at you in the previous exercise. For the key-employee resignation crisis at work, the real problem is a lack of resources to support the growth of key employees.

For the flat-tire crisis at home, the problem there is chronic burnout. I'm not saying a flat tire in this scenario isn't frustrating and stressful—but the fact that it threw off your entire week tells me the tire, the car, and the kids' schedules—while frustrating—aren't the main issue. It's the "messed up your entire week" part that's the real problem.

Now that your solutions team, at work or at home, knows the real problem, they can create a long-term fix.

Create and Implement a Long-Term Plan

It's important to note here that you'll still be around and accessible to your team at this point. You can answer questions when asked. But the actual creation and implementation of the longer-term plan to solve the real problem? Delegate it. Give your team what you have and then let this work go (for now). Part of their long-term plan will be for them to check in with you at certain milestones and on some decisions. But other than that, let it go.

At this point, you've battled burnout. You've made space to address it, learned about its different types and identified your own, and isolated it, and now the problems it's caused are being handled by your team. You've learned a lot through this process thus far, and now you're ready to move into the next stage: recovering personally from burnout.

CHAPTER TAKEAWAYS

Burnout can cause problems, and problems can cause burnout. Either way, these immediate problems must be addressed. The business owner's first step is to assemble their solutions team.

- Addressing the problems surrounding burnout is a two-part approach. First, develop and implement a quick-fix plan to stop the crisis in its tracks—to stop the spiral. Once the quick-fix plan is in place, the solutions team can then plan and implement the long-term fix.

- You'll be involved during the quick-fix plan, but you should delegate the creation and implementation of the long-term strategy to your team.
- Addressing and fixing the problems around burnout is not the same as recovering from the toll that it's taken on you. Once the long-term strategy is handed off to your team, you can start to personally recover from the burnout.

CHAPTER 8

Recover from Burnout

Now that you're on the other side of the urgent fire, it's time for you to focus on personal recovery. Entrepreneurs sometimes think that once the problems surrounding it are addressed, burnout goes away. What often gets overlooked is recovering from the personal toll burnout takes.

Addressing the crises burnout creates, which we did in the last chapter, is not the same as your personal recovery.

Recovering from burnout looks different for everyone. From the amount of time you need to what you find will work for you—all of that varies.

For some, making big changes is how they recover from burnout.

THE SABBATICAL

Prior to becoming a Martha Beck Certified Wayfinder,[10] Angie Stegall helped business owners with their processes and organization. But there came a time when that didn't feel right. She wasn't happy, and she knew she needed to change her business. What followed was a six-year journey to recover from, and then leverage, the burnout she had experienced.

Part of the journey included a sabbatical from work for a year and a half. Both Angie and her husband are business owners, and at that time they were beyond burned out. I'm not exaggerating when I say the burnout experience can cause an entrepreneur to close their business. Luckily for Angie's clients, the sabbatical was a break from business, not a goodbye.

As Angie describes it, "By the end of 2016, my husband and I had both been self-employed for over a decade each. He was mentally and physically falling apart after ten years in construction. I was so sick of marketing, sales, the grind, and serving clients that weren't in alignment with me." Angie knew something was off, that something had to change, and then she took it a step further.

She recalls, "I looked at my husband and said, 'Let's shut it all down.'" At first, her husband didn't think they could do that, but Angie was right there to say, "Oh, yes, we can." They sold almost everything they owned, bought an RV, and traveled the country. They worked for a surveying company as subcontractors for a while and ultimately ended up in Alaska for a summer.

While she was on her sabbatical, Angie practiced a lot of techniques to make space. She did keep a few clients, but she said no to new in many ways. She also was very clear about the only business initiative she was interested in continuing: getting her Wayfinding accreditation. Those *were the only two work-related items she kept on her plate. Everything else was open space for her to recover from burnout.*

Recovering from burnout is about personally regaining what you've lost and setting the table to leverage your experience to your advantage (which we'll cover in chapters eleven and twelve). You are a limited resource. Burnout means you are being depleted faster than replenished. This chapter is all about replenishing *you*.

In this chapter, you'll decide how to utilize the space you've made to recover from burnout. You'll learn how to create a personal recovery plan. Along the way, you'll build momentum to launch you into preventing and leveraging burnout.

Chapter Overview

Section	Summary
Step 1: Recall Types and Note Signs Step 2: Prioritize by Type of Burnout	In the first two steps, you'll recall the types and signs of burnout and prioritize them in a unique order.
Step 3: Identify Possible Actions for the Least Painful Type of Burnout	You'll then identify some options to help you recover from burnout. This section provides questions and guidance to narrow down the list.
Step 4: Select One or Two Actions for Each Sign Step 5: Implement	These steps will help you select the self-care actions you'll implement with a few questions. You'll also learn how to make sure you implement these recovery actions.
How Will You Know When You've Recovered from Burnout?	You'll learn how to quantify your recovery.

Let's get into the steps of your personal burnout-recovery plan.

STEP 1: RECALL TYPES AND NOTE SIGNS

The first step in personally recovering from burnout is to identify the types of burnout (attentional, emotional, and physical) you're experiencing, along with the signs of each type you've noticed in yourself. In chapter five, I described some of the signs for each type and offered questions you can ask yourself to help you figure out which ones you're experiencing.

If you haven't yet worked through the exercises in chapter five, please do so now. There is no right or wrong number of signs. If you're overwhelmed, pick only the top three signs you've most recently experienced.

Knowing your type(s) of burnout will help you make decisions in the following steps to make your personal recovery more efficient and effective.

Now that you have your list of types and signs, we can move on to prioritizing burnout recovery by type.

STEP 2: PRIORITIZE BY TYPE OF BURNOUT

I said this earlier on in the book, but it's worth repeating here—the last thing I want is for your burnout-recovery plan to cause more burnout!

This step helps focus your recovery efforts so that the process doesn't cause more stress. I recommend prioritizing the types (attentional, emotional, and/or physical) from which you need to recover.

How to Prioritize Your Burnout Types

In this example, I'm going to assume you're dealing with all three types (attentional, emotional, and physical). Review the signs and red flags you're experiencing for each type.

Then, ask yourself the following questions:

- Which type of burnout (attentional, emotional, and/or physical) is hitting you the hardest?
- For which type are you seeing fewer signs or experiencing less pain?

Order your types of burnouts from "least painful" to "most painful." *Pain* and *suffering* are subjective terms, and only you can decide which type is causing you the least and the most amount right now.

You'll begin your personal recovery by working on your "least painful" type of burnout.

Why Are We Prioritizing from Least to Most Pain?

I ask you to start with the least painful type of burnout for several reasons:

- **Quick wins.** Recovering from your least painful type is often easiest to accomplish. You'll get a "quick win" in this part of the process. These quick wins are like kindling that can fuel the rest of your recovery.
- **Snowball effect.** You'll work on the other types that are causing you more pain with some momentum, confident that you can do this work.

- **Crawling before walking.** Biting off more than you can chew at this point will almost certainly keep you from recovering fully because you won't work the process.
- **Gaining experience.** Recovering from the type of burnout that's causing the least amount of pain will teach you lessons that can help make recovering from the other types of burnout a little easier.

Now you have your types of burnout prioritized in a list from least to most painful. You also know the signs of each type you're experiencing. Let's now identify some ways to help you recover.

STEP 3: IDENTIFY POSSIBLE ACTIONS FOR THE LEAST PAINFUL TYPE OF BURNOUT

In this step, you'll identify recovery options that will work for you for your least painful type of burnout. This step is about identifying options; we'll make a final selection from the list of options in an upcoming step.

You're still going to protect the space you made back in chapter four, but now you'll use some of that space to recover from burnout.

Before you start making this initial list, make sure you read the rest of the instructions for this step. Often, business owners get overwhelmed at the idea of "Put it all on the list!" The following filters will help you determine which burnout-recovery actions you realistically have at your disposal right now.

"Will Work for You" Filter

What constitutes "will work for you" actions? You probably have an idea of activities that fill up your fuel tank and those that drain it. You know what comforts you and what does not. You also know the state of your other resources. "Will work for you" means something you can do right now or reasonably soon. Budget, upcoming family events, world events, your work calendar, your current physical abilities, and other factors need to be considered when making this list.

Know Thyself

Meghan Lynch is an introvert, and she needs alone time to recharge. "When I was burned out, I felt constantly empty, and I knew I needed alone time to recover from that burnout." In Meghan's case, what works for her to recover from burnout is to spend time alone. The activities that help her recover are likely dramatically different from what an extrovert may do.

The "will work for you" filter has two elements to it. First, you gauge if an action is something that will restore and replenish you. Second, you consider if you can implement it within the next thirty days.

If you can't do it within the next month, it doesn't pass through this filter.

This is one of the many reasons vacations don't work for business-owner burnout. While, yes, taking a vacation to recover may work sometimes, it's usually not doable within thirty days for a variety of reasons. Planning a vacation can cause more stress as well!

You may think I hate vacations, but it's quite the opposite. They have a time and place when it comes to burnout. The key to incorporating vacations effectively in this context is to make them part of your prevention strategy (we'll discuss this in chapter nine).

So what kind of activities and resources are you looking for? Known (or educated-guess) self-care and comforts.

Known and Educated-Guess Comforts That Will Work for You

When you're personally recovering from burnout, you don't want to recreate the wheel. If you know meditating helps you, it goes on the list. If walking is an activity that reduces stress for you, it can go on the list. If therapy works for you? Book an appointment. Does a really cold bedroom help you sleep better? Adjust your thermostat. These are known comforts that you already know work for you.

If you find that your known comforts won't address your type of burnout or aren't accessible right now, you'll need to make some educated guesses about what might work. Educated-guess comforts are new-to-you self-care activities based on your known comforts.

For example, if meditating works for you, but you feel like you need more movement in your self-care to recover from your burnout, yoga might be a good educated-guess activity. If a cold bedroom helps you sleep but your air conditioner is on the fritz and you can't replace it right now, using a fan and sleeping with no blankets may be an educated guess to try.

Wherever possible, this recovery-action list needs to include mostly known actions that you've done before. For some of us business owners, though, trying something new helps us recover (even if it turns out we dislike it). Aim for 80 percent known comforts on this list and leave space for 20 percent educated-guess comforts.

The "will work for you" filter will be unique to you, as will your known and educated-guess comforts. Let it guide you as you identify possible activities.

STEP 4: SELECT ONE OR TWO ACTIONS FOR EACH SIGN

From the list of possible "will work for you" actions that you can implement within the next thirty days, you'll now select one or two for each sign of the type of burnout you're working on right now. If you have a lot of signs, you may want to pick only one action item for each. On the other hand, if you have only one sign for this least painful type of burnout, you may want to select two options to address it.

For example, if you're dealing with attentional burnout, your signs may include a lack of focus and inability to make decisions. For each of those signs, you'll want to identify one or two recovery actions. Having the same action for each sign is fine (this crossover is encouraged). Meditation helps me with both focus and decision-making. Look at that efficiency!

As you work through this section, remember to only do this for the signs of one type of burnout at a time. You start with your least painful type of burnout. If you're experiencing more than four signs of the type of burnout you're working through in this step, you can further prioritize those signs from least to most painful.

Here's an example template of how this step works for a couple of signs of each type of burnout.

Your type of burnout (attentional, emotional, or physical)
Your signs (up to four) of this burnout and selected "will work for you" actions to address each:

- Sign one: selected "will work for you" actions to address this sign
- Sign two: selected "will work for you" actions to address this sign
- Etc.

Suggestions for Choosing Your Options

If you find yourself in a position where you have a lot of options, that's a good thing! It means you've taken some time to try self-care in the past and know what works for you in certain circumstances. But there's a downside to a lot of options—you have to choose. To help you make your choices, here are three ideas to guide you.

Look for Crossover

You may find that the same self-care action helps address multiple signs of your burnout. You may even find that when you work through this exercise for your other types of burnout, a self-care action that helps an emotional-burnout sign can also help with a physical-burnout sign.

If one action, like taking a nap or exercising, helps multiple signs and/or multiple types of burnout, that may be an ideal choice.

Stick with Your Most Known

If you find yourself with many options, select the options you are the most familiar with because they will be the easiest to implement. You won't have to do any research. You probably already have any tools you need (walking shoes, meditation app, etc.). You also know how much of your own resources, like time, energy, and money, you'll need to invest to implement those items.

Speed and Impact

Speed and impact can also help you decide which self-care actions to select. For example, if setting boundaries about challenging conversations takes less time than it does to hang out with friends, focus on setting boundaries. The faster you can begin to implement one of your actions, the more quickly it will help you recover from burnout.

If walking has a bigger positive impact on you than napping does, choose walking. If an action takes a little longer to implement or become a habit, but the positive impact of that action on your burnout recovery will be quite large, that's also a consideration.

Remember, you want to begin to implement these actions within thirty days, so use that time frame to help you decide as well.

Now let's work through each type of burnout so you can see this process play out.

Attentional Burnout

Signs of attentional burnout may be that you struggle to make decisions and you lose your train of thought easily when speaking to your team at work.

Possible self-care actions that have helped you make decisions more easily in the past could include making a pros-and-cons list, breaking decisions down into much smaller pieces, and talking to other business owners you trust about impending decisions. If you want to add an educated guess here, journaling may also be a self-care action that can help you with your attentional burnout because you already know that making lists helps you.

When it comes to the burnout sign of losing your train of thought when speaking to your team, actions that have helped you in the past may include writing down the key points you want to make ahead of a meeting and rehearsing what you'll say. If you're looking for an educated-guess action you could take here, you could consider having another team member lead your meetings.

Based on selection criteria and past experience, this is how the completed template might look:

Your type of burnout: attentional
Your signs of this burnout and selected "will work for you" actions to address each:

- Struggling to make decisions: discuss with peer groups and break down decisions into smaller ones.
- Losing train of thought when addressing team: write down key points before meetings and rehearse what to say.

That's just one example of making a list for two signs of attentional burnout. Your signs will be different, but the process is the same. Remember, you're looking for "will work for you" actions first. If needed, you can then include educated guesses.

Let's now look at how this would work for two signs of emotional burnout.

Emotional Burnout

When you're in emotional burnout, you may struggle with self-confidence or be irritable with those around you.

Actions that have helped you regain self-confidence in the past could include reviewing glowing testimonials of your work, hanging out with friends, going to therapy, and practicing gratitude. In addition to that, an educated-guess action might be to better understand imposter syndrome by reading a book about it. You now have a list of known comforts, as well as one educated guess, to add to your recovery list for emotional burnout.

For the emotional-burnout sign of irritability, you may have previously found that setting boundaries about unexpected and unpleasant conversations—in both your personal and work lives—helps a lot. That might sound like, "I know this conversation is important, but I need to schedule it for a later time." This gives you time to prepare and be more open for the conversation, even if you're still struggling with irritability.

Other actions that may have helped you through irritability might include taking an impromptu nap or exercising. If an impromptu nap has helped in the past, scheduling naps would be an educated-guess comfort you could try.

Make your selections and note your actions in the same template as above or in the free workbook you can claim at https://www.the juliebee.com/burned.

Now that we've worked through an example of making a list for emotional burnout, let's do the same once more for the final type of burnout: physical.

Physical Burnout

Let's say physical burnout shows up for you as poor sleep and lower-back pain.

Actions that have worked for you in the past to address poor sleep due to burnout could include meditating, taking a medication to fall asleep, reading a fiction (nonbusiness) book before bed, exercising, and cutting back on caffeine. If you're looking for an educated-guess activity, you might add journaling—if meditating and reading work, journaling might be effective, too.

Actions that have helped your lower back feel better in the past may include going to your chiropractor once a week, walking, and using an app to remind you to get up from your desk every thirty minutes to move. If you want to add an educated guess, a standing desk may help. Or, if you like chiropractic care, getting a massage may also work. These would be good educated guesses based on what you already know.

Your List Is Ready!

You've identified your list of self-care actions to begin your recovery journey from the type of burnout that's causing you the least amount of pain right now.

I know you want to recover from all three types as quickly as possible, but walking through all three types with the examples above illustrates why working on all of them at one time might create more burnout instead of helping you recover from it. It's a lot to consider all at once. Doing it this way (one type at a time) will be more manageable and provide quick wins to ignite a spark that keeps you going.

You may be thinking right now that there's no way you can do everything on the list you've made—even with the space you created in chapter four. The good news is, you don't have to do *everything* on your list of actions to recover; I just think it's nice to have options to choose from at this point. Armed with your possibilities list, you're ready to move forward.

STEP 5: IMPLEMENT

To recover from burnout, you'll use some of that space you created in chapter four. You've used that space for quite a lot at this point. Each chapter in this book requires you to use some of that space, but once you work through it, you get that space back to continue along with this guide.

Now you're going to use some of that space for implementing the self-care items you selected in the previous step. This is all about taking care of *you*.

Plan It

It's easy to say, "Put it on your schedule." What they don't tell you in adulting school is that it takes a bit of time to actually put something on your schedule. This requires thoughtful planning.

For example, if you decide hanging out with your friends is a self-care activity you will implement, you'll reach out to your friends and ask them to hang out. Then you have to plan where to go and what to do. Then you'll all need to find a time that works for most of you. Scheduling an activity on your calendar isn't the first step in planning; it's closer to the end of planning for most things.

Even if it's a solo activity, like exercising or taking a nap, it still requires some planning before you can schedule it. For exercising, you may need to get a new pair of shoes or join a gym. For napping, you might need to consider how long you will nap and when you will do so.

For almost every example that can be planned, you'll also want to consider how often you want to do that activity.

Planning is thinking through the things you'll need and what you want before you schedule something. This distinction between planning and scheduling is a subtle but important one.

Schedule It

Now that you've planned the activity, you schedule it. I recognize that at this point you may feel overscheduled. Some business owners can plan to do a self-care activity and fit it in when it works for them. If scheduling doesn't work for you, this step can be less structured.

For others, including myself, putting something on my calendar is a great accountability tool. I know I've made space for the activity; so does my team and my wife (they can see my calendar). If I put paddleboarding on the calendar, I can guarantee I will be asked the next day, "How was paddleboarding?" There's a baked-in accountability factor for people who live by their calendars.

Whether you decide to put an activity on your calendar or opt to keep it less structured, the important outcome here is that you use some of that space you created in chapter four to do your self-care activities.

I also recognize there are some things that can't be scheduled, like enforcing boundaries around unexpected and unpleasant conversations. When these conversations arise, you could ask to schedule them for later and not have them right then and there. Or you could decide to approach the conversations when the timing feels right.

Again—whatever works for you. The important part is that these recovery actions happen.

Do It

Easier said than done. If you struggle with this part, an accountability partner may help. Those people who have supported you throughout the process? Those are the people to ask for help with accountability in this stage. You can ask them to check in with you about the activity or for help in seeing it through. For example, if exercise is a self-care activity, you could ask a friend to exercise with you. The people you've relied on throughout the steps in this book are the people you should turn to and ask for accountability help.

You can work out what that looks and sounds like with them. They just need to know how they can support you in performing these self-care tasks.

Repeat

Most of these self-care actions are ones that recur (exercising, napping, scheduling time to think, etc.), though sometimes you'll have a self-care action that doesn't repeat, like getting a medical test done that you've been putting off for a while. You'll continue to do these self-care activities (and anything that supports your doing them) until you feel like you've mostly recovered from this type of burnout. Some of these activities will also make it into the prevention plan (more on this in chapter nine) so you may continue doing some of them even after you recover.

Repeat Steps 3–5 for the Next Prioritized Burnout on Your List

All right! You're implementing your self-care actions to recover from burnout. Kudos! The self-care actions you take may become part of your ongoing plan to prevent burnout. Or you may do them less frequently or not at all. We'll cover that in chapter nine.

Once you're done implementing the self-care steps for your least painful type of burnout, you move on to the next type of burnout on your prioritized list, repeating steps three, four, and five. If you're experiencing all three types of burnout, you would do this process three times.

If you're only experiencing one type of burnout, your work inside this chapter is complete. You are, most likely, not fully recovered from burnout yet, but you're working your plan to get there. You can always return to this chapter for more insights or in the case of a future burnout.

HOW WILL YOU KNOW WHEN YOU'VE RECOVERED FROM BURNOUT?

If you have not yet completed the baseline-to-burnout exercise in chapter two for your red flags, now would be a good time to do so. The way you know you've recovered from burnout is by noting when you get back to baseline for those measurable red flags.

Let's look at sleep as a quick refresher. I need an average of seven hours of sleep each night; that's my baseline. I hit burnout if I get five hours or less of sleep on weeknights for two consecutive weeks. My danger zone is in between those two markers. I know I'm recovered (or almost recovered) from burnout if I'm getting an average of seven to nine hours of sleep most nights each week because that's my baseline "normal" range.

Once you're recovered from burnout, you'll be ready to learn how to build a prevention plan. To prevent burnout, you cannot be actively burned out. If you are, working through the recovery steps in this chapter is crucial to eventually build a successful burnout-prevention plan.

CHAPTER TAKEAWAYS

Recovering from burnout personally is an important step in the burnout-battling process. It's about taking care of yourself to replenish what burnout depleted.

- When recovering from burnout, take it one type (attentional, emotional, or physical) at a time. Start with the type that's causing the least amount of pain. Tackling this one first builds confidence and experience, giving you a quick win to keep you going.
- For each sign of this burnout type, you'll identify and select self-care recovery actions to implement. When determining which actions to implement, stick to known comforts that will work for you. If there is crossover in your recovery actions, that's an added bonus!

- If you struggle to implement the self-care recovery actions you select, ask for help from your support team. Let them know what you need help with and how they can hold you accountable for performing your self-care actions.

Part III

MOVING FORWARD AFTER BURNOUT

CHAPTER 9

Prevent Future Burnout

A question I'm asked fairly often by business owners is, "If burnout is unavoidable and I need to embrace it, why have a prevention plan in the first place? Why not stop at the recovery plan?"

A lot of burnout is preventable, but sometimes it's not. While preventing every case of burnout may not be possible, having the awareness to catch it early, and then a plan in place that keeps it from spiraling further, is possible in most cases.

Not all burnout has to fully deplete you or set you back. Even for the unavoidable cases, a plan can help you prevent them from burning your business (or you) to the ground. Remember what I said in earlier chapters—a person does not go from great to burnout overnight. No matter where you are in your red-flag danger zone, this chapter can help you work to prevent full-on burnout.

In this chapter, you'll document your stories of past resilience, define boundaries for your work and personal lives, and create a list of resources you can turn to when you feel you're approaching burnout. After completing the work in this chapter, you'll have a four-step burnout-prevention plan that you can integrate into your everyday life.

Chapter Overview

Section	Summary
Step 1: Create Your "I'm Resilient" Folder and Review Monthly	What the "I'm Resilient" folder is, why it's important for preventing burnout, and what to include within it.
Step 2: Define Your Ideal Workweek	How to identify your ideal workweek within the realities of business ownership, with examples.
Step 3: Define Your Ideal Personal Life	How to find work–life harmony by defining your ideal personal life and what elements to include, and deciding how you want to show up outside of work.
Step 4: Identify Resources for Help (Before You Need Them)	The three categories of resources to have, examples of resources, and why you want to build this structure now.

STEP 1: CREATE YOUR "I'M RESILIENT" FOLDER AND REVIEW MONTHLY

The first step in preventing burnout is to remember and document your own burnout history—the stories of your past experiences. I call this the "I'm Resilient" folder.

Your folder can also include stories about other challenging times in your life, even times before you started a business. Your resilience skills started well before your business did. Before you knew what burnout was, you knew what stress felt like. You overcame it. Those challenging life experiences go in this folder, too.

When we go through hard times, we often want to forget those difficult moments in our lives. To bury them. To pretend they didn't happen. Who wants to remember some of their hardest moments?

I'll tell you exactly who—entrepreneurs who want to prevent future burnouts. The moments that live in your "I'm Resilient" folder document your ability to overcome, move on, and grow from those experiences.

This folder is a living document. It's not something you compile once and then ignore. You'll add your stories to your folder after every burnout or deeply challenging time you experience. You'll start to see patterns emerge. Prior stories will help you move through future challenges, fatigue, and periods of disengagement.

As for the creation of your "I'm Resilient" folder, the great news is that you don't need to write that much about each difficult moment.

In practice, you may keep this information in a computer file folder, with one document for each burnout. Some business owners keep a journal. Others may keep notes using online software or an app on their mobile device. You can find a template for this in the workbook, available as a free download on my website: https://www.thejuliebee.com/burned.

However you normally take notes—that's the way to do this exercise. Just be sure to give your folder its own separate space from your other notes.

What to Document in Your "I'm Resilient" Folder

What kind of information goes into your "I'm Resilient" folder, exactly?

For each burnout or challenging life experience, you'll want to answer these questions:

Question	Guidance
When did the experience begin and end?	If you're unsure, you can use estimates. What you want from this answer is a general sense of how long this experience lasted.
What and who were the precipitating factors?	See chapter six on identifying causes. Heads up, the answer to this question might be you.
What types of burnout did you experience, and what were your signs of it?	Remember, the three types of burnout are attentional, emotional, and physical. See chapter five for help identifying their signs.
What did the experience cost you, both personally and in your business?	I've heard answers like productivity, financial security, staff, peace of mind, marriage strain, depression, imposter syndrome, and so on. There are many costs to burnout, both tangible and intangible.
How did you recover from the experience?	Even before you had this book, you knew some ways to help yourself recover from massive stress. Recall and note as much as you can remember.
What did you learn about yourself and your business?	This is where you begin to leverage your experience; we'll talk more about that in the remaining chapters of this book. For now, just note the major lessons you learned, both about yourself (always applicable) and your business (if applicable).

Answer those questions for two or three of the most memorable stress-inducing moments in your life. These could be recent or from earlier times in your life—as far back as your teenage years.

Most founders write about one page for each experience. Remember, you're the only one who's going to see this, so let loose. Don't worry about grammar, spelling, or (if you're like me) horrible handwriting. All that matters is that you can read and access your answers.

Later, you can go through this practice with other experiences. For now, having two or three experiences documented is all you need.

How Often Should the Folder Be Reviewed?

I recommend you schedule a time to review your "I'm Resilient" folder at least once a quarter; I review mine once a month. It's much easier to recognize, prevent, or even overcome burnout if you know you've done it before. With this folder, the proof of your resilience is right in front of you! It will help you maintain your self-confidence, no matter what. Sometimes you just need a reminder, and this folder delivers it. I've found that receiving this reminder about once a month helps me immensely, especially in troubling or uncertain times.

If your folder has quite a few stories in it, you don't have to review every story each time you review it, but don't avoid reviewing the especially hard ones. Sometimes the hardest moments teach us the best lessons.

Why Is This Important to Do?

First, it gives you a better understanding of what burnout looks like on you—which is crucial. Going through this exercise feeds the rest of your prevention plan because it helps you begin to identify patterns, boundaries you didn't have but created after that moment, and resources that were helpful in your time of need. It can also help you further flesh out your red flags and triggers, as discussed in chapters two and three.

Second, it's cathartic—it helps you see and feel that you have gotten to the other side. It reminds you that you've emerged from the ashes of burnout. That you can move forward because you've done so before. That you learned something from these experiences while you played with the flames. You may have been burned—scorched, even—but you survived.

Third, it gives you a resource to go back to when you start to feel burnout heating up again. The past does repeat itself, and nowhere is that truer than in our own histories. Sometimes saying, "Hmm, this reminds me of that one time . . ." and then reviewing the notes from that time can help you act sooner.

If you have your history documented, it can help you see a burnout coming and start taking action to lessen the impact. It can also help you prevent the burnout before it even starts.

Now that you've documented a couple of your past difficult times, we're going to work on how to prevent or minimize burnout in the future. You'll do this by defining your ideal circumstances, both in your work life and your personal life. You'll also document resources that can help you so that when you need them, you'll already have them prepared.

STEP 2: DEFINE YOUR IDEAL WORKWEEK

It's crucial for business owners to define their ideal workweek because that helps them create boundaries. Self-made CEOs need work boundaries to prevent burnout. Without boundaries, work will fill every ounce of every day, if they allow it to do so. Defining their ideal workweek helps entrepreneurs set those boundaries and reclaim some space for themselves.

A note on workdays: In my examples, I tend to stick with the Monday–Friday workweek framework. Not everyone has the same perspective; I know many founders who look forward to going into a quiet office on a Saturday morning to work.

I do, however, believe it is important to have at least one full day off from work in the seven days that make up our week, no matter which day you prefer, so please keep that in mind.

To Define Your Ideal Workweek, Answer the Following Questions

- On what days of the week will you work, and at what times?
- When will you work on the big-picture, visionary topics each week?
- When will you invest time with your staff?
- When will you do the tasks you do not enjoy?
- What is your ideal state of mind at work? Calm, collected, and happy to be there?

Allow yourself some flexibility here. If you find answering these questions overwhelming, just answer the two that are easiest for you to answer right now.

After you answer these questions, you'll have some great boundaries around your ideal workweek. I recommend you review your answers once a week at first. After you successfully implement these workweek boundaries for a month, you can review your ideal work-week answers less frequently. If you find yourself breaking these boundaries, you may need to review more frequently.

Examples of Ideal Workweek Boundaries

Some general examples of ideal workdays may include being in the office, or leaving the office, at a certain time each day. If you work from home, like I do, it may involve leaving your home office and closing the door by a certain time.

I often see entrepreneurs experience burnout because they are constantly putting out fires, working on the urgent but not import-ant tasks, and rarely getting to those visionary-level tasks. Those big-picture, strategic tasks are very important but usually not urgent. However, those are the tasks that will move the business forward toward its vision. When a founder feels like they can't get to those tasks, this will often lead to attentional and emotional burnout.

A boundary I believe every business owner needs is scheduled time, at least twice a month, to work on visionary items. You might log out of your team communication tool, or possibly not go into the office during that time, to limit distractions.

Another possible boundary is having your week scheduled one week in advance and not allowing people to schedule last-minute appointments within a week. That depends on you, your company, and what you want your ideal workweek to look like.

If you are extroverted, you may need to go to one networking event a week to be around other business owners. If you are introverted, maybe your ideal workweek does not include networking events; that may be more of a once-a-month adventure for you, after which you do not plan other work because you'll need time to recharge.

An example from my own experience illustrates how I define boundaries between work and personal life during my ideal day at work. I do not respond to texts or phone calls from family while working. I read the texts or listen to voicemails, but I don't respond during the workday unless it's an emergency.

Finally, the state of mind you are in while at work is a big part of your boundaries. For me, I prefer to show up at work calm, focused, and open to ideas. Do I show up that way every day? No. Some days are hectic and frantic. I do have an awareness of when I show up in my ideal way and when I do not. When I don't, I make a mental note and focus on respecting this boundary the next day.

These are just a few examples I have heard and experienced over the years. What's important is that you create your ideal workweek and then practice it.

Will every day be ideal? No. The point of all this is progress, not perfection. If you notice you are successfully practicing your ideal workweek two out of five days per workweek, whereas before you didn't even have a definition of your ideal, that is massive progress! Maybe the following week your goal becomes three out of five days. Again, progress, not perfection.

Now that you have your ideal workweek better defined, let's look at your ideal personal life.

STEP 3: DEFINE YOUR IDEAL PERSONAL LIFE

Your ideal personal life is just as, if not more, important than your ideal workweek. I suggest identifying your ideal workweek boundaries first because those are often easier to define for business owners than are boundaries in their ideal personal life. The boundaries you set around your workweek will enable you to have the capacity for your ideal personal life.

There are even more options when it comes to your personal life. As a general rule of thumb, however, I prefer to have entrepreneurs work with what they already have access to right now or can have access to within the next month or two.

If you're working toward something you want in the future—for example, to compete in a triathlon or to become an expert at a hobby—include steps that will get you to that future in the burnout-prevention plan we're forming in this chapter.

In this step, you will draw your best life and then live it a little bit at a time.

There is no one-size approach to this; what's important is that you invest some time into thinking this through and writing it down. Here are a few thoughts to get you started.

Ideal Personal-Life Elements to Review

When structuring your ideal personal life, you'll want to include some (or all) of these elements:

- How you want to show up as a friend, spouse, child, parent, etc. (Look at all the other roles you play in life besides being a company owner.)
- Nonwork activities and hobbies you already practice or would like to pursue, and a plan to do them regularly.
- Time and a plan to take care of your well-being, like time to exercise and go to doctor appointments.

- Personal-development activities, like reading, reflecting, and meditating.
- Planned vacations—even if these involve just staying home and not doing work.
- Time with family and friends.
- A morning routine you practice most days, including what time you wake up.
- Evening and bedtime routines you practice most days, including what time you turn out the lights for sleep.
- Any other boundaries that you'll use to keep work from invading your personal life.

If addressing all of these is overwhelming, select three to start with and build from there.

Living an Examined Life

Angie Stegall is a big fan of living an examined life. When I asked her how someone begins to live an examined life, she said, "Ask yourself: What are you tolerating now? What do you feel obligated to do? Obligations and tolerations are a great place to make some space." This is also a great way to identify what needs to be reduced or removed when you define your ideal personal life. You could also use this same strategy when defining your ideal workweek.

Examples of Ideal Personal-Life Elements

Sometimes it's hard to get started on this exercise, so here are a few examples to help you.

When it comes to defining how I want to show up as a partner to my spouse, I want to be present. I want to laugh with her. I want to listen more than I talk. I want her to feel supported by me. I do not want to think or talk about work on the weekends or when we are on vacation.

When it comes to hobbies, many business owners have a hobby outside work but struggle to make time for it. It might be that, in your ideal personal life, you have time for your hobby once a week—maybe you work on your hobby every Thursday evening. No matter what, set some time aside for that hobby. If this is a struggle for you, try to find a hobby you can easily do at home.

In my own life, I love to paddleboard, but until I live on a lake, it's an all-day affair to go paddleboarding. It cannot be my only hobby. I've recently started whittling, which is something I can easily sit down and do for fifteen minutes in the evening at home.

All the business owners I know who have a good work–life harmony have worked very hard to have a personal life. They set strong work boundaries and communicate them with the people who matter to stay accountable.

To keep work out of my personal life, one boundary I have is to put away my phone when I'm with my family, friends, or wife. I'll keep it in my bag, and sometimes I'll even leave it in my car if I think the temptation to check emails and Slack will be too great.

Once you define your ideal personal life, you practice living that definition. Having a focus on living your ideal personal life will keep your work life in check. In a way, defining your ideal personal life is the ultimate accountability for keeping those workweek boundaries you set in the prior step.

Now that you've gone through these steps to form a burnout-prevention foundation, we're going to identify resources to help you.

STEP 4: IDENTIFY RESOURCES FOR HELP (BEFORE YOU NEED THEM)

Have you ever been overwhelmed and someone asked how they could help, but you had no idea how to answer? Were you unsure of what to even ask for?

That's why this is part of your prevention plan. When you're approaching burnout, or you know you're already in it and don't know what to do, you want to have an existing list of resources that can help.

Resources List

In general, these resources will fall into one of three categories; sometimes, there's crossover. The categories are health and well-being, entertainment, and help from others. I suggest having two or three resources in each category. For example:

Resource Category	Examples
Health and well-being	Monthly therapy, weekly exercise, and daily meditation.
Entertainment	Watching a favorite TV show, hanging out with a friend, reading a book, and working on your hobby.
Help from others	Hiring a monthly house-cleaning service, having your significant other take over dinner duty, and asking your leadership team at work to hold you accountable for leaving the office at a certain time each day.

When relying on others, make sure these individuals are aware they are part of your resource plan before you call on them for help.

Remember, these are resources to help prevent burnout. You may already be taking advantage of some of these resources, but if you feel like you're approaching burnout, you might want to increase their frequency.

A Few Resources That Have Helped Business Owners Prevent Burnout

A team that can be asked for help. A vacation fund. A therapist, doctor, and psychiatrist for medical attention. Entertainment, like a YouTube channel that makes you laugh. Improv classes. A friend to hang out (and not discuss work) with. Passes for local parks. A gym membership. A business coach or mastermind group full of people who understand the business-owner journey. Caregiver backup.

There are countless options, but whatever or whomever holds you accountable to your work boundaries, facilitates your ideal personal life, and helps you prevent or recover from burnout—those resources go on this list.

Whatever you put on this list, you'll want to have them set up and ready for activation before you need them. It's hard to find a new psychiatrist or therapist when you're in the middle of never-ending stress. Joining a gym can seem overwhelming for someone going through extreme fatigue. Even texting a friend and trying to explain what's going on can be daunting in the thick of difficult moments.

Have that support structure already set up so that you don't have to seek it out when you need it—it'll be just a quick phone call, email, or text away. Then—and here's the easy part—use those resources when you need to do so!

BURNOUT-PREVENTION PLAN SUMMARY

Congratulations! If you have worked through this chapter, you are a business owner who now has a complete burnout-prevention plan. All the steps in the prevention process play an important role.

It seems like a lot of information now, but the more you practice some of these elements, the more positive habits you'll form to prevent burnout. You'll find that some of the burnout red flags and triggers from chapters two and three will become easier to handle. The structure you've added to your ideal personal life will become second nature. The boundaries you've set for your workday will become your normal. At a certain point, you may not even notice when you're following the prevention plan, but you'll notice when you begin to deviate from it. That's when you'll know you've mastered burnout prevention for business owners—identifying when you are off course and knowing how to get back on track.

And now we can move on to the really fun part of burnout: how to embrace and leverage it!

CHAPTER TAKEAWAYS

The foundation to a burnout-prevention plan includes honoring your resilience, setting boundaries, and then creating a resource list you can turn to when you feel burnout approaching.

- Your "I'm Resilient" folder is a crucial part of your burnout-prevention plan. The stories you document will highlight your ability to overcome, move on from, and grow from those challenging experiences.

- Defining your ideal workweek helps you set boundaries around work so that it doesn't take up every free minute you have to spare. Defining your ideal personal life then helps you identify how you want to show up, live, and be outside of work, which provides structure to an often unstructured part of life.

- Finding help in moments of need is often overwhelming. By compiling a list of resources now to help you prevent burnout later, you will be better prepared when you need that help. The help will be easier to ask for and receive.

CHAPTER 10

Embrace Burnout

Now that you've recovered from burnout and created a pre-vention plan, we can start moving forward. I believe burnout is inevitable for most entrepreneurs. Even if you have a great prevention plan (which you created in chapter nine), circumstances can appear out of nowhere that will cause you to burn out. At some point in our careers as CEOs, we will face burnout. What I think is most important here is that we recognize this and accept it without feeling guilty or beating ourselves up when it happens.

I also know that burnout can have a positive impact on us. If we pay attention to what we learn throughout the process or review it in hindsight, we'll often find a silver lining. Nearly every entrepreneur I've spoken to who has experienced burnout came out the other side with several valuable lessons.

Some founders take this a step further, though, going beyond lessons and experiencing full-on breakthroughs that help them become better, more successful humans (however they define success). But how do they do it? The ones who leverage burnout most successfully do two things differently than the rest—they embrace the burnout (instead of only surviving it), and they identify the breakthroughs and brainstorms they had during the recovery process and then act on them.

In this chapter, you'll learn how to embrace burnout through a simple (and very effective) improv rule. I'll also share a three-step process to help you play with the fire without getting burned. This chapter is essential work to leverage burnout, which you'll learn more about in the following chapters.

Chapter Overview

Section	Summary
Embracing Burnout	Why it's important to embrace burnout, and one simple rule that will help you do so.
Playing with the Fire	How to get closer to the fire of burnout to examine it and understand more about what happened.

EMBRACING BURNOUT

How in the world does someone embrace burnout? I fully recognize how counterintuitive this sounds. Accepting that you're burned out is one thing, but embracing it? Embracing goes beyond radically accepting a situation as is. Embracing means that you accept a situation and decide to welcome it into your life.

Why would I suggest that business owners welcome burnout into their lives? Because it helps us drop our own guilt surrounding it. Once we drop the guilt, we can then look up and see those silver linings and lessons. Embracing burnout enables a founder to see the big ideas again, to learn the lessons from it, to have breakthroughs, and to make the most of the experience. This sounds great, but how does one actually do this?

To embrace burnout, there's only one rule you need. It's called "Yes, and . . ."

"Yes, and . . ." Explained

"Yes, and . . ." is a comedy-improv rule. It's also one of the best ways to embrace just about anything challenging in life, including burnout. In improv, "Yes, and . . ." simply means you take whatever your cast-mate gives you and build on it.[II]

Improv Example in Action

When you're in an improv skit, you want to support whatever your scene partner serves up to you. For example, say your castmate starts an improv skit with, "It's weird we're on this boat, right? I mean, if a friend asks you to help them move, you help them move. But it's weird he's moving . . . here."

Then, it's your turn to take that and build on it with, "Yes, and . . ." The possibilities are endless. "Yes, it is weird we're on this boat, and I think the move is good for our friend. I just have no idea where he's going to keep his pet llama / store his expensive artwork / deal with his motion-sickness problems / sleep in a canoe." (Your castmate didn't say what type of boat it was!)

It's "Yes, and" something. You accept what your castmate gives you and take it further. They will then, in return, do the same. Round and round it goes until the emcee calls, "Scene." In this example, you would *not* say, "Well, we're *not* on a boat—we're in his ex-wife's apartment" or, "It *is* weird we're on a boat, but we're helping him learn to sail, not move."

How does this apply to business-owner burnout?

"Yes, and . . ." in Burnout

To move forward after burnout, the first step is to embrace that you went through it in the first place. Own it. Name it. That's the "Yes" part of the rule as it applies here. Then you approach it with a "Yes, and . . ." mentality. Here's what that might look like:

> Yes, *I experienced horrible burnout,* and *I learned [fill in the blank] about myself. I know that's important, so I'm going to dig into that to see what breakthroughs I might uncover.*
>
> Yes, *I dealt with the crisis the burnout caused,* and *I am now personally recovering from it. While I was dealing with the crisis, I discovered [fill in the blank] about my business. I took note of it while addressing the crisis, and now I'm ready to explore the possibilities.*

By embracing burnout with the "Yes, and . . ." approach, you'll begin to recognize those serendipitous signs and moments that tend to show up when we're at our lowest of lows. Now is the time to review them.

What Embracing Burnout Can Do for Your Business

Looking back on her sabbatical, Angie Stegall says, "It was the best thing we ever did. Everything changed for the better." That sabbatical was Angie and her husband's "Yes, and . . ." moment. They embraced that they were burned out and needed a radical change. They then discovered how they could leverage it to embody their definitions of success.

When they made their way back to North Carolina in 2019, Angie was an accredited Wayfinder and ready to coach her clients on their own journeys. Her husband had also identified his passion—wildlife conservation photography—and began attracting clients for his photography business.

Today, Angie reports that she's had her most successful years ever in business since returning to North Carolina as a Wayfinder. "Taking that time off from being a business owner helped me get radically clear about wanting to be a Wayfinder. During our sabbatical, we had time to rest, play, get creative, revisit hobbies, and sit and do nothing. We healed ourselves in many ways."

That's the power of burnout. Yes, it sucks—*and*, if you look for those silver linings, you may have a breakthrough that changes you and your business in profound ways.

"Yes, and . . ." is the first step to embracing burnout. It's the step that helps you begin to see your difficult experiences in a positive light. As a business owner, you will find that this positive reflection on your experience is crucial to the next part of embracing burnout: playing with the fire.

PLAYING WITH THE FIRE

Now that you've noted some positive outcomes from your burnout, you're going to set the stage to leverage it and fuel your success and growth. To do that, you'll need to play with the fire of burnout without getting burned.

Step 1: Name Your Feelings About Burnout

I'm not going to ask you to experience your feelings; naming them will suffice. As you've learned, simply naming burnout, and owning that you've gone through it, validates the experience. So name those feelings! Anger, frustration, excitement, disappointment, competitiveness, being fired up, sadness, enlightenment, awareness—whatever it is, name it.

You also don't need to say *why* you had these feelings; just note what feelings you had. For example:

- This burnout made me angry.
- It made me feel like a loser.
- It made me frustrated.
- It made me aware I micromanage.

If you struggle to name your feelings, sometimes naming how you felt physically is a good place to start. For example:

- This burnout exhausted me.
- It made me sick to my stomach sometimes.
- It made me break out into cold sweats.
- I had muscle knots in my neck that wouldn't go away.

I normally suggest limits on work like this, but this is one place where I believe it's important to get it all out. Write all those feelings down and say them aloud. Are you feeling a little heat at this point? It can sometimes be hard for founders to do this part of the exercise because it can bring back up the swirl of burnout—which is like playing with fire. When I get into those swirls, here's a mantra that helps me—think of it like a fire extinguisher:

That was then; this is now.

You are not back in that burnout experience; you're simply unpacking how it made you feel.

Once you've done this, you're ready to move on to the next step.

Step 2: Remember Your Personal Values and Note Misalignments

The next step in playing with the fire of burnout is to remember your personal core values and note any misalignments that stood out during your burnout experience.

Your Personal Core Values

Some of us inherently know our personal values; some don't. They are at the core of what makes it possible for you to fall asleep at night. They are the essence of what makes you you. These are not the same as your company's core values. While there's usually overlap between a business owner's personal core values and those of their company, they're still two separate sets of values.

Some examples of core values include loyalty, openness, freedom, compassion, competitiveness, abundance, vibrance, trust, authenticity, harmony, and integrity. There are many! Write down your top three core values—the core values that, if you were out of alignment with them, would cause you to struggle to sleep at night.

If you don't know your core values or if you need to redefine them, that's okay. Identifying your core values could be its own book. The fastest way to identify a list of core values is to review a list of values on the internet and pick three. Later on, once you've started leveraging your burnout, you can dive deeper into your core values. I've shared my own process in the bonus workbook you can receive for free (see instructions in the introduction), but I suggest you not start that journey until after you complete the burnout work within this book.

Note Any Personal Values Misalignment That Led to the Burnout

This is where business owners become very aware that they are getting close to the flames of their burnout—but don't worry, you won't get burned. Keep repeating that fire-extinguisher mantra: That was then; this is now.

Getting Close to the Fire

Meghan Lynch is very aware of one of her core values: "One thing that's critically important to me is making an impact. Success for me is feeling like whatever I'm doing . . . is valuable to someone. I don't have a specific definition of the type of impact I need to have; I just need to feel like what I'm doing matters."

A lack of impact, that misalignment with Meghan's core value, was one element that caused burnout. "We were working with huge companies," she says, "but I didn't feel like we were making an impact. Once we transitioned Six-Point Creative to working with family-owned businesses, we could see the impact that we made on those businesses. We could also see the impact those businesses made on their employees and their local communities. That is what is important to me."

When Meghan completed the culture-gap exercise and found the gap included values misalignment, Meghan was playing with the fire of

burnout. She was very honest with herself and her role in the burnout,
identified a values misalignment, planned to address it, and then imple-
mented that plan. To leverage a burnout, we can play with the fire of
it—getting close to it but not being burned. This helps us gain even more
clarity about what happened.

To identify values misalignment, you can start with the list of feelings you created in step one and then compare that to your personal
values identified in this step. Are there any obvious misalignments?
Here are a few examples.

One of your core values might be compassion. One of your feelings from step one is that the burnout made you feel like a loser.
Considering someone else a loser isn't compassionate, and the same
applies to you. Considering yourself a loser means you're lacking
compassion for yourself. That's a values misalignment.

Or say that, from step one, we learned the burnout made you feel
frustrated. Maybe one of your core values is gratitude. Being frustrated often comes from only seeing what you lack, not what you
already have. Frustration that comes from failing to recognize what
you have is out of alignment with gratitude.

One more example, and then we'll move to the final step in this
chapter. Let's say the burnout made you feel like there will never be
"enough." One of your core values is abundance, or an abundance
mentality. Wondering if you have "enough" comes from a place of
scarcity, which is the opposite of abundance.

If you struggle with the feelings part of this process, I get it.
Another option to replace the feelings section is to look at decisions
you made during the burnout. Compare these decisions with your
core values and look for things that were out of alignment.

By the end of this step, you will probably have at least one values misalignment between how burnout made you feel or caused you to act and your core values. This is often a hard activity for business owners to go through for many reasons, but it's a necessary one. Raising awareness of core-values misalignment helps us not only leverage burnout but also see it coming in the future. If you feel you're out of alignment with your core values at any point in time, you may be in the danger zone, sliding toward burnout.

When you master the skill of values alignment, your answer to the question in the next step—"Could you have seen it coming?"—will frequently be yes. Let's move on to the final (and hottest) step in playing with the fire of burnout.

Step 3: Could You Have Seen It Coming?

And this is where you get as close to the flame as you can without getting burned. This is where you're gliding your finger through the flame of a match without lingering long enough for it to hurt.

Ask yourself, "Knowing what I know now, could I have seen this burnout coming?" This question is not meant to make you feel bad about your past actions. It is meant to help you learn lessons you see now that you didn't see then; this will help you prevent burnout in the future.

How do you answer this question? You review the work you did in steps one and two above—evaluating your feelings or decisions, core values, and misalignments—before answering this question. If you had paid closer attention to your building frustration, could you have seen the burnout coming? If you had noticed the misalignment between your feelings during that time and your core values, could you have seen the burnout coming? No one else needs to know the answer to these questions. We know that hindsight is 20/20, but we also know that history repeats itself. Answering these questions honestly helps you learn from your past, avoid repeating your mistakes, and grow smarter from the lessons you've learned along the way.

"Could I have seen this coming?" is an uncomfortable question to answer but a necessary one. This is the question that makes you wiser about burnouts in the future. If diving into it feels too hot, you can practice this skill with mistakes instead—those that didn't push you over the edge. I believe this practice of examining our past and learning from it is an important skill.

Some burnouts you really can't see coming—those are often the acute ones. It may be that the answer to this question is "No, I couldn't have." But chronic burnout usually has warning signs. Many of them come from values misalignment that you can pay attention to and address going forward. Once you've answered this question honestly, you can move forward as a more informed business owner.

Now that you've done the hard work through these steps to embrace burnout and play with the fire, it's time to reap the rewards. You'll next learn how to leverage it!

CHAPTER TAKEAWAYS

The improv rule of "Yes, and . . ." is the way to embrace burnout. First a business owner acknowledges that, yes, they experienced it. Then they determine the "and" part of the equation, which helps them gain more insights about their experience.

- Name your feelings about the burnout. If naming feelings is too challenging, it's okay to substitute feelings with decisions you made during that period.
- Then, consider your personal core values. Look for any misalignments between how the burnout made you feel, or the decisions you made during that time, and your personal core values.
- Ask yourself, "Could I have seen the burnout coming?" Answering this question will help prevent future burnouts and will also help you leverage what you discovered in the most recent one.

CHAPTER 11

Leverage Burnout

Leveraging burnout can bring great success to you and your company. By the time you get to this point, you've gone through quite a lot. You've had a lot of moments of awareness, self-reflection, frustration, excitement, relief, and everything in between. You've also learned how to prevent getting to this point again. For some, that's enough.

But for some, it isn't. You may find that you go through an experience like this, and when you get to the other side, you ask, "What's next?" High achievers are always reaching for new milestones. Passion-fueled entrepreneurs aren't often satisfied with the status quo.

My perspective on burnout as a founder is this—if I'm going to go through it, I'm going to make sure I learn something that can help me be a more successful person on the other side. That "more successful" part is what it means to leverage your burnout.

In chapter ten, you learned why you should embrace burnout with open arms instead of running away from it. Running away from fire is a natural response. But when it comes to a business owner's struggle with never-ending stress and fatigue, only you can put that fire out. The more comfortable you become with standing inside the ring of fire, the more you'll be able to leverage your burnout experiences.

In this chapter, all the work you've done thus far culminates in an opportunity to leverage your burnout experience. This chapter provides a structured plan to help you identify leverage points from your burnout experience and shows you how to make permanent space in which to pursue those leverage points, igniting a spark that will fuel your success and growth.

Chapter Overview

Section	Summary
Step 1: Make Permanent Space	How to convert some of the temporary space you made in chapter four into permanent space for your leverage points.
Step 2: Identify Your Possible Leverage Points	What leverage points are, where they come from in this process, and how to create a list of possible ones.
Step 3: Select One Leverage Point to Pursue	Why you select only one leverage point, and guidance on how to narrow down your possible leverage points until there's only one left.
Step 4: Leverage Burnout	Three crucial points to consider to ensure your leverage point will succeed and how to work through them.

How to Leverage Burnout

"In order to rise from its own ashes, a phoenix first must burn."
—Octavia Butler

In many ways, the business owner's journey through burnout is like that of a phoenix—the mystical bird that catches fire and turns to dust, only to be reborn from the ashes and fly to even greater heights than before. You can't have a comeback without a setback. Without burnout, you cannot leverage it. That's the silver lining of this entire experience. Here's how you harness and leverage what you've learned throughout this process.

STEP 1: MAKE PERMANENT SPACE

There are two sparks that we can use for leverage. These sparks come from what you've already done in this process and bring us full circle in that ring of fire.

The first spark is permanent space. In chapter four, we talked in depth about making temporary space to address your burnout. Throughout this guide, you've used that space for various activities and work to address, recover from, and prevent burnout. At this point, some (or perhaps most) of that space should still be available to you.

Now you will turn some of that temporary space into permanent space. You will permanently stop doing at least one item you temporarily stopped doing throughout this process. Yes, permanently. It might be a task someone took off your plate while you've walked this path—a task that you've discovered they handle better than you ever did. It might be a few tasks of a caregiver role you play. It might be a part of your morning routine that you stopped doing and realized you don't miss.

Exit a Business and Start Another: An Example

Today, Travis Rosbach has taken all that he's learned as an entrepreneur and funneled that into the Tumalo Group. He discovered his leverage point—what he is very passionate about—once he reviewed his past burnout stories and experiences. "I love business—I love doing business," he explains. "I'm passionate about helping others do business and about bringing manufacturing back to America. I'm doing work I love." So while Travis had his brush with the downside of fame after selling Hydro Flask, he's no longer dealing with burnout, and he leveraged the lessons learned to build a new business he loves.

I can hear the busy entrepreneur in you resisting this thought. "How can you expect me to stop doing the work I've done in the past? The plan was always to temporarily pause or delegate that work, not to permanently drop it!" This is true. The plan was for some work to temporarily be removed from your plate.

But humor me for a minute. You haven't done those tasks for a while now—do you *really* need to pick them back up? Can the solution you set up to get those tasks done while you were addressing and recovering from burnout become a permanent one? The answer to that question won't be yes for everything you've delegated, eliminated, or put in a "later" pile. Some of that work will come back onto your plate. But there will be at least a few things you should now see that you don't need to do.

How Do You Determine What to Permanently Stop?

Go back to the lists you created in chapter four. Review the to-dos you took off your plate, whether that was through temporary delegation, elimination, or just a pause.

Ask yourself these questions:

Question	Things to Consider
Can the person who took this over for you keep it on their plate?	If the answer is yes, permanently delegate it.
Does it make a difference if this task gets done or not?	It's possible that when you eliminated that task for a short period, no one seemed to miss the outcomes. If the answer to this question is no, permanently eliminate it.
Does this task align with your core values?	If this is work that falls outside your core values, try to delegate or eliminate it. Doing work that is out of alignment can cause burnout.
After going through burnout, does this business initiative you paused make sense to continue?	Sometimes you'll learn lessons during this journey that help you realize a business initiative is just not right for you or your company.

This is not an exhaustive list of questions, and you can come up with some of your own to help you discern and decide what needs to permanently go for you to protect the space you've created.

Some of the items you paused or moved around to make temporary space will need to be put back on your plate, but not all of them. If no one (including yourself) missed your work on those tasks, or if someone else did them well, there's a good chance you don't need to bring that work back into your space.

This can be an overwhelming thought for some founders, so take it slow. It requires courage and bravery to admit to yourself that work you were doing in the past no longer needs to be done by you (and maybe doesn't need to be done at all). Identify two to four items to explore here. You can always change your mind and take them back, if needed.

This is the time to create permanent space in your life because you've actually already created it! Now it's time for you to own it. It is on you to set boundaries and protect them. And oh, will you want to protect this space, because we're about to dive into the second spark that will help you leverage burnout.

You're going to pursue a new initiative, one that is in line with your personal core values. We'll call these initiatives leverage points.

STEP 2: IDENTIFY YOUR POSSIBLE LEVERAGE POINTS

In every part of this work, you likely had breakthroughs, "aha" moments, and epiphanies. Remember how I told you early in the book to make a note of any silver linings or ideas that popped up? Now is the time to get those notes out. These ideas can arise at any point in the burnout process.

Some of those ideas were passing thoughts that you noted but then moved on from. Not all of them, though. Some of them stuck with you throughout the process. There are probably a few ideas that, once you thought of them, you couldn't unthink. Those are the leverage points to bring back to the table here. This is the second spark that fuels growth.

You may have thought things would go back to "normal" once you got to this part of the book. But that old "normal" doesn't exist anymore. It can't exist in the same way, because if it did, you would continue to burn out.

You are now a wiser business owner who has recovered from burnout, addressed the crisis of it, and made a prevention plan. You have created permanent space for this breakthrough. Now is when you get to explore it.

Your burnout leverage point is the idea or breakthrough you'll pursue using the permanent space you've made.

STEP 3: SELECT ONE LEVERAGE POINT TO PURSUE

Why pursue only one leverage point?

First, founders like shiny, new objects. If you are like most, you've probably had several breakthrough ideas as you've worked through this book. If you pursue more than one of them, though, you may end up back where you started—with too much on your plate and burned out. By eliminating two to four items permanently, and only replacing them with one item, you'll accomplish two things:

- You'll make permanent space.
- You'll retain some of that permanent space because you'll only be pursuing one leverage point.

Getting Back in Alignment

Meghan Lynch's leverage point was recognizing that her company, Six-Point Creative, was serving clients that did not align with her core values. As she'll tell you candidly, "We went from working with Fortune 500 companies to family-owned businesses." She hasn't looked back since and has found immense success in working with those family-owned businesses. Just as importantly, she also discovered the role she needed to play in her company.

"I needed to get myself into that visionary role instead of doing the work," she says. "I love brand strategy, but I had to let that go. I recognized my role was to be the leader, the visionary, and set my team up for success. And let me tell you—they just kill it these days." Meghan had two leverage points that fueled her company's success—all while remaining aligned in values and fostering a fantastic workplace culture.

I've said several times throughout this book that the last thing we want is for a burnout-recovery process to cause more burnout. Selecting one "aha" to pursue is how you ensure that pursuing your breakthrough doesn't lead to more burnout.

I Had Several "Aha" Moments—How Do I Choose Only One?

In this scenario, there's usually one breakthrough idea that you can't stop thinking about. It's become a constant companion. It lights you up. You're falling in love with it. However, you have other good ideas that may make more sense for you to pursue.

So how do you know which leverage point to pursue? Here are three tactics to help you decide which to pursue and which can wait for a later time. There are no hard-and-fast rules here, just guidance. Your ultimate choice is one you'll pursue and live with, but these tactics will help you figure it out.

Wonder and Wander

To wonder, try to think that anything is possible. Anything. Dream your biggest dreams here. Then wander—get outside, play, paint, write, or go somewhere you can move around. Wander without agenda. When I do this, I think differently. I'm able to make connections between thoughts and ideas that were previously unconnected. This tactic always helps me when I get creatively stuck on big ideas.

How Will Each Leverage Point Help You?

When determining which leverage point to pursue, answer the following questions:

- How will this enrich your life?
- How will this elevate your company?
- How will this enhance your community?

Keep the answers short, maybe up to three sentences for each leverage point in consideration. Whichever one has the most potential to inspire you, to light you up—that's the one to pursue. It isn't about the scale and size of the potential here; it's about what ignites your soul.

Pursuing a leverage point that ignites your soul—that is in alignment with your core values—will fuel your growth and success (however you define them). This is what helps you become a better human.

Trust Your Gut

Finally, when considering which leverage point to pursue, trust your gut instincts. A gut instinct is hard to describe because it varies so much from person to person.

For me, I know I'm on the right path when I experience an ebb and flow between a calm, settled feeling and an excitement about what is possible. I also know I'm on the right path when I have no frustration about the leverage point I'm considering or the fact that something new and likely challenging lies ahead.

My only explanation for this, beyond "gut instinct," is that whatever idea I'm considering is in full alignment with my core values. If you know who you are at your core, your gut instinct becomes a lot stronger.

That's my experience with my own gut instincts. Yours may be similar or wildly different. The one thing I know for sure about gut instincts, though, is that they are rarely wrong. If you're struggling to select a leverage point from burnout, trust your gut.

STEP 4: LEVERAGE BURNOUT

This is the culmination of everything you've learned throughout this book. You know the leverage point you will pursue. It could be a new business or a new service or product. It could be changing an entire process. It might be a new life in a new city. It could be an equally significant personal leverage point, like seeing your extended family more frequently, planning several vacations for the next two years, or starting a new self-care routine.

Because you've worked through the layers of burnout, you are equipped to decide how you will leverage it. You get to make that call—you've earned it.

Purpose Found

Frank Schwartz leveraged the lessons he learned from his burnout in two ways. First, he found his personal purpose, which is to help people remove their self-limiting beliefs so they can uncover their personal purpose and find success in their areas of influence. From there, he founded G3L Leadership, where he lives his personal purpose every day.

If we pay attention and look for the silver linings in burnout, breakthroughs happen.

How does one actually leverage burnout, though? It starts with a plan. The plan at this point can vary greatly from person to person, depending on the leverage point. But each plan to leverage burnout usually starts with three elements.

First, you have a brainstorming session about the leverage point. This could be with your team at work or with your family at home. It may be an individual brainstorming session.

Second, you do a top-level gap analysis. Note where you are and the resources you have today, where you ultimately want to end up, and what you need to fill in the gap between the two. More detailed plans and timelines can come later.

Third, you determine if the leverage point is feasible based on the gap analysis. For example, for a business-feasibility analysis, you would want to know if the leverage point will add value to the business in some way (profit, efficiency, reduced stress for everyone, a better culture, etc.) and if it's realistically possible to close the gaps.

For personal leverage points, it's about identifying resources to fill any gaps and the likelihood you'll be able to use those resources. Examples of this might be the availability of classes to learn a new hobby or determining if that two-week vacation to Hawaii is financially realistic within a set time period.

If the leverage point passes through this final check, it becomes a new initiative and you go into strategic-planning mode. If the leverage point isn't feasible, you can return to your list of possible ones from step two and go through the brainstorming, gap analysis, and feasibility study again.

You are now prepared to leverage the burnout you've overcome. You've earned this moment. Plan it, implement it, and succeed! Someday you'll look back and say, "This [fill in the blank with something amazing] would never have happened had I not leveraged my past burnout!"

CHAPTER TAKEAWAYS

To leverage burnout, you'll transform some of the temporary space you created in chapter four into permanent space. You'll use that permanent space to leverage what you've experienced and learned.

- Your leverage points are ideas that came from breakthroughs or "aha" moments you had while working through the other chapters in this book. Most business owners have several potential leverage points they want to pursue, but to avoid another burnout, you should only pursue one.

- To determine the one leverage point to pursue, there are a few tactics you can use. You can wonder and wander, ask yourself three questions to determine how a leverage point might help you, and trust your gut.

- Creating a plan to leverage burnout starts with brainstorming, a gap analysis, and a feasibility study to set up your leverage point for success. After that, you further plan and strategize, and then you implement!

CHAPTER 12

The Gift of Burnout

You made it! You've learned so much throughout this book—
pat yourself on the back. You now have the tools to prevent burnout
and also to address it when you cannot prevent it. You've created
boundaries for yourself, you know what red flags to look out for, and
you have a slew of other tips, tools, and insights to help you succeed
in your ventures, even when facing the flames of burnout.

I do want to note one final element because I think it's important.

THE ULTIMATE GIFT OF BURNOUT

Burnout helps you become a master at prioritizing based on many
factors: work–life harmony, your core values, your strengths, and
what you enjoy doing. Because of that sharpened prioritizing skill,
burnout teaches you how to identify what is a "Heck yes!" and what

is a "Not in a million years" when you face challenging decisions at work and in your personal life. It gives you the clarity to know those answers.

Getting to the other side of burnout also builds your resilience, capacity, and confidence. It gives you new perspectives. It broadens your comfort zone by pushing you outside it. It even builds your credibility as a leader.

All these benefits can help you become a more successful human, at work and in your personal life, no matter how you define success.

They say fortune favors the bold.

I also believe that fortune favors those who embrace and leverage burnout.

ACTION STEPS SUMMARY

This book can serve as a source to return to whenever you need it. When I read process-focused books, I appreciate a short summary of all the action steps I need to take. For your reference, here are all the steps we covered in one place. These are also included in the workbook you can download from my website (see the introduction for details), with more examples and stories to help you implement them.

1. Burnout Is Different for Business Owners and Why This Matters
   a. Of the six reasons burnout is different for business owners, have you experienced any of them? Which ones?
   b. Have you ever felt stuck in your business because of burnout?

    c. How has your burnout affected those around you, both at work and at home?

    d. Look for silver linings as you move through this book.

2. Burnout Red Flags

    a. Determine your burnout red flags (not sleeping well, being unable to make a decision, etc.) and identify a way to measure them.

    b. Determine your baseline (your "normal"), burnout level, and danger zone for each red flag.

    c. Determine one or two action steps you can take when you're in your danger zone to stop the slide into burnout.

    d. Determine how you will remain aware of your red flags. If you need support in this, ask for help from an accountability partner.

3. Burnout Triggers

    a. Identify your burnout triggers (other people, places, or scenarios).

    b. Categorize your triggers into ones you can eliminate, ones you can limit, and ones you cannot limit.

    c. Eliminate whichever triggers you can.

    d. Decide how you will interact with triggers you cannot eliminate entirely.

4. Make Space to Address Burnout

    a. Say no to new.

    b. Pause any business initiatives that you can.

    c. Document your to-do list for your business and personal life.

    d. Sort your list into "eliminate," "delegate," and "later."

    e. Prioritize your remaining to-do list. Ask for help with prioritizing, if needed.

    f. Work the plan.

5. Identify Burnout Types and Timelines

    a. Determine if you are burned out; the four indicators covered in this chapter and the MBI assessment can help.

    b. Determine your type of burnout (attentional, emotional, or physical). You may be experiencing one, two, or all three types at the same time.

    c. Determine your time frame of burnout (acute or chronic).

    d. Begin to see what is good about burnout.

6. Determine Causes and Isolate Your Burnout

    a. Identify the causes of acute and chronic burnout.

    b. If you have chronic burnout, get away from the stress zone, identify the stressor and what you think or feel about it, then ask, "Why?" three times to help you identify the underlying cause of your chronic burnout.

    c. Isolate how and when you talk about burnout from other conversations by recognizing the words you use to discuss it.

    d. Isolate your burnout thoughts from your other thoughts by noting when you think about burnout and then getting back to what you were thinking about previously.

7. Address the Problems Burnout Creates

    a. Ask for help and assemble your solutions team.

    b. Create and implement a quick-fix plan to stop the burnout from spiraling further.

   c. Observe and review learnings from the quick-fix plan's implementation, including a team debrief.

   d. Delegate the creation and implementation of a long-term plan to your solutions team.

8. Recover from Burnout

   a. Recall your types of burnout (attentional, emotional, and/or physical) and their signs.

   b. Prioritize your burnout by type, from least to most painful. Start with the burnout type causing the least amount of pain.

   c. Identify "will work for you" recovery actions.

   d. Select one or two self-care options for each sign of burnout.

   e. Plan, schedule, do. Repeat these steps if you're dealing with more than one type of burnout.

9. Prevent Future Burnout

   a. Create your "I'm Resilient" folder.

   b. Define your ideal workweek.

   c. Define your ideal personal life.

   d. Identify resources for help in protecting your boundaries (before you need them).

10. Embrace Burnout

   a. Embrace burnout with a "Yes, and . . ." approach.

   b. Play with the fire of burnout by naming your feelings about it and remembering your personal values.

   c. Note any core-values misalignment that caused burnout.

   d. Ask if you could have seen it coming.

11. Leverage Burnout

   a. Make permanent space out of the space you made in chapter four.

   b. Identify possible leverage points (opportunities).

   c. If you have more than one possible leverage point, wonder and wander, name possible benefits of each, and trust your gut. Select one leverage point to pursue.

   d. Leverage the burnout—brainstorm, perform a gap analysis, check for feasibility, and then get to work!

12. The Gift of Burnout

   a. What gifts have past burnouts given to you?

   b. What will you do with those gifts now that you have a better understanding of burnout for business owners?

EPILOGUE

What Happened After the Emergency Room?

Leaving the emergency room that evening after my panic attack, I knew something had to change. I knew what could immediately change and what would take time. I also felt an immense amount of guilt because I knew I was burned out, I hadn't done anything about it, and my burnout had affected everyone around me.

A few weeks later, I had started to make necessary changes. I'd also identified that, as a business owner, I needed to approach burnout differently going forward for the sake of myself, my companies and the people who work for me, and my personal relationships. Instead of merely reacting to it, I determined that I would need to proactively address burnout before it occurred. Over the years, I'd come up with tactics to help myself prevent and overcome burnout, but what I was lacking was a system to keep me accountable for using those tactics.

I needed a reference guide I could turn to when I felt stress starting to become burnout. That guide became this book, which documents an entire system. The funny thing is that I'd already practiced everything that ended up in this book. I had a system. I just hadn't been using it as a complete process because I didn't have it all in one place.

As I talked with other business owners about burnout, I realized that many of them had very few resources to deal with the stress and overwhelm in their lives. Compared to what was available for the general population, there were fewer resources, fewer definitions, and just less of everything. There was no real guidance specifically for them.

It was far past time for us to have a guide for burnout. I wanted to help business owners prevent it and address it as it happens.

It was then that I decided to embrace burnout instead of running from it. To make it productive. To plan for it. To leverage it. This line of thinking felt very empowering for me. Courageous, even. Different. Bold.

Publishing this book was my leverage point from that burnout.

BURNOUT AWARENESS WHILE WRITING THIS BOOK

I wrote this book during a time when I was flirting with my burnout danger zones on a regular basis. There was a lot going on in my life and my businesses. I went through a major editing process while a key team member resigned at work. I finished this book between hospital rooms and a rehab center as I took on caregiver duties for my dad, who was recovering from several strokes. If I hadn't actively worked the plan outlined in the system I share in this book, I would've burned out.

This book would never have been written if I hadn't used the system it provides. It's only because I had the awareness of where I was in my journey that I was able to leverage that time in my life to write this book.

I know burnout is hard. I think it's inevitable, especially for business owners. I believe that it's only once we accept it as a part of our world and our lives that we can really leverage it.

If you picked up this book, I'm guessing my story resonated with you in some way. I want to normalize burnout conversations, and sharing my own stories with you is one way to do that.

Burnout is often the greatest spark you can receive, and now you have a road map for how to leverage that spark into something fantastic. Work the system. Look for those silver linings. Find your leverage point. Let burnout ignite something in you that you haven't felt before. Something big, something awesome.

Something that starts a fire in you—in the best ways possible.

ACKNOWLEDGMENTS

I've read acknowledgments in many books. Writing this now, I have deep empathy for those authors who have written them. There are many people I want to thank, and it is inevitable that I'll miss someone. I ask for your forgiveness in advance if your name doesn't appear here, and I promise to make it up to you in my next book.

A book takes a tribe, and I thank mine here.

Marcy—my wife, my partner, my ride or die. Thank you for your unwavering and constant support, for *always* believing in me when I didn't believe in myself, and for your patience with me on all things business. Your compassion and grace are only outmatched by your love.

Jessica Heatly—thank you for always believing in me, calling me out when needed, encouraging me, and being the bestest best friend. Our summits are some of the best times I've had in life, especially when attempting dramatic readings of obscure industry publications or eating sushi. Your early work in the developmental stages of this book set it up for success. Tycoon!

Angie Stegall—thank you for your years of coaching, mentoring, and guiding me. For holding space for over a decade so that this idea could develop and be born. The encouragement you gave me in those years of finding my creativity will never be forgotten. Thank you.

Michelle O'Connor—thank you for your support and reassurance over the years. Your willingness to brainstorm ideas with me, your positive and critical feedback on everything I send your way, and the way you always show up are all priceless. I treasure our friendship. Thank you.

Lee Anne Moore—girl, we have been through some stuff. Thank you for taking my mind off work like no one else can. Honestly, three hours with you feels like a trip to Disney World. I never know what we'll get into, but I know we'll laugh until our faces hurt doing it. #2facery #harmonizingladyvoices #faafo #thankyou

Trish Saemann—thank you for allowing me to share your stories in this book. Your vulnerability is refreshing; your kindness, humor, and generosity are uplifting. Thank you for believing in me. You probably don't know this, but your support, specifically in 2021, sustained my own belief in this manuscript. Thank you.

Chris Melton—thank you for starting a podcast for me even though I didn't want one. You saw something that I didn't see in myself. That podcast turned into so many other projects, but it also validated that my words make an impact. Thank you for making me sound great. Also, thank you for your friendship.

Matt Holt, Katie Dickman, and the team at BenBella and Matt Holt Books—thank you for believing in me and this manuscript, for giving this topic a platform, and for your guidance along this journey. I'm proud to call myself one of your authors. Publishing has more twists and turns than I ever imagined; I'm so glad I've had you to plot the course, allowing me to do what I do best—create, teach, and connect.

Mom, Dad, Valerie, Chris, Jacob, Hannah, Hayley, and Ashley—thank you for loving and supporting me even when you aren't quite sure how to explain what I do for a living. You can now tell everyone I'm an author!

Jeff, Ayisha, Connie, Michael, Luca, the Van Brunt crew, and Rob—thank you for all of your support, cheerleading, and photography (Jeff). I married into a wonderful family that loves me and is proud of me no matter what. You'll never know how much that means to me.

There are many others who either helped make this book come to life or inspired and motivated me in some way, and I thank them here:

Frank Schwartz, Travis Rosbach, Meghan Lynch, Debbie Peterson, Lena Lumelsky, Rebecca Kitson, William McKee, Diona Kidd, Renee Hode, Mary Brown, Stacey Randall, Helen Ruth Harwell, Ann Marie Sunderhaus, Laura Holt, Caryn Lee, Paige Armstrong, Scott McIntosh, Eileen Schlesier, Katie Parker, Linda Smith, Daniel Winegarden, LeeAnn Shattuck, Sharai Lavoie, Fabi Preslar, Nesha Pai, Cassmer Ward, Marcelo Plaza, Melissa Froelich, and anyone who has shared their burnout stories with me over the years. Thank you all.

Finally, to the business owners who bought this book looking for a solution to burnout: I see you, and it's gonna be okay. Thank you for investing in yourself, and I look forward to hearing your stories of how you leveraged burnout!

ENDNOTES

1   Sangeeta Bharadwaj Badal and Jennifer Robison, "Stress and Worry Rise for Small Business Owners, Particularly Women," Gallup, May 26, 2020, https://www.gallup.com/workplace/311333 /stress-worry-rise-small-business-owners-particularly-women .aspx.

2   "Small Business Outlook: Long-Term Confidence Amid Headwinds," Capital One Insights Center, October 12, 2022, https://www.capitalone.com/about/insights-center/small -business-outlook-fall-2022/.

3   Georgia McIntyre, "What Percentage of Small Businesses Fail? (And Other Need-to-Know Stats)," Fundera by NerdWallet, November 20, 2022, https://www.fundera.com/blog/what -percentage-of-small-businesses-fail?.

4   "Burn-Out an 'Occupational Phenomenon': International Classification of Diseases," World Health Organization, May 28, 2019, https://www.who.int/news/item/28-05-2019-burn-out -an-occupational-phenomenon-international-classification-of -diseases.

5   Christina Maslach, Susan E. Jackson, Michael P. Leiter, et al.,
     "Maslach Burnout Inventory™ (MBI)," Mind Garden, 1981–2016,
     accessed February 12, 2022, https://www.mindgarden.com/117
     -maslach-burnout-inventory-mbi.

6   Alexandra Michel, "Burnout and the Brain," Association
     for Psychological Science, January 29, 2016, https://www.
     psychologicalscience.org/observer/burnout-and-the-brain.

7   Sherrie Bourg Carter, "The Tell Tale Signs of Burnout . . . Do
     You Have Them?," *Psychology Today*, November 26, 2013, https://
     www.psychologytoday.com/us/blog/high-octane-women/201311
     /the-tell-tale-signs-of-burnout-do-you-have-them.

8   "What Is Burnout?," Cleveland Clinic, February 1, 2022, https://
     health.clevelandclinic.org/signs-of-burnout/.

9   Melinda Wenner Moyer, "Your Body Knows You're Burned
     Out," *New York Times*, February 15, 2022, https://www.nytimes
     .com/2022/02/15/well/live/burnout-work-stress.html.

10   Martha Beck, "Wayfinder Life Coach Training," Martha Beck
     website, accessed May 15, 2022, https://marthabeck.com/life
     -coach-training/certification/.

11   David Alger, "Rules of Improv I," Pan Theater, accessed February
     10, 2023, https://pantheater.com/rules-of-improv.html.

ABOUT THE AUTHOR

Julie Bee isn't just an award-winning entrepreneur—she's been dubbed the "small business fixer" by her clients and peers. With over 15 years in the entrepreneurial field, Julie has solidified her reputation as a dynamic consultant, a riveting speaker, and a leader who sheds light on the darker side of business ownership. She has a knack for transforming businesses from the ground up. Whether it's reshaping workplace cultures or empowering leaders, her influence proves game-changing for those who collaborate with her. Having been celebrated by Fast Company and Forbes, her insights are in high demand across the industry. If you're searching for a groundbreaking guide, explore what Julie offers at thejuliebee.com.

Join Julie on her mission to help one million entrepreneurs prevent burnout and achieve success!

Subscribe to her weekly newsletter for tips, tools, exclusive offers, and inspiration that will help you thrive as a business owner.

thejuliebee.com/newsletter/